Robert William Duff

The herring fisheries of Scotland

Robert William Duff

The herring fisheries of Scotland

ISBN/EAN: 9783743341821

Manufactured in Europe, USA, Canada, Australia, Japa

Cover: Foto ©ninafisch / pixelio.de

Manufactured and distributed by brebook publishing software (www.brebook.com)

Robert William Duff

The herring fisheries of Scotland

International Fisheries Exhibition

LONDON, 1883

THE

HERRING FISHERIES

OF

SCOTLAND

BY

R. W. DUFF, M.P.

LONDON
WILLIAM CLOWES AND SONS, LIMITED
INTERNATIONAL FISHERIES EXHIBITION
AND 13 CHARING CROSS, S.W.

1883

International Fisheries Exhibition,
LONDON, 1883.

CONFERENCE ON THURSDAY, JUNE 28, 1883.

DR. LYON PLAYFAIR in the Chair.

THE HERRING FISHERIES OF SCOTLAND.

IN the paper I am about to read on the Herring Fisheries, I do not propose to discuss the natural history of the herring, as that is a subject which at these Conferences, and elsewhere, has been amply dealt with by far more competent authorities.

I propose to treat the Herring Fisheries from a practical point of view, showing the progress of the industry, its national importance, and the requirements for the maintenance and further development of the most productive Fishery of the United Kingdom.

A knowledge of the natural history and habits of the herring is doubtless necessary for the proper treatment of the subject, even from the point of view I am attempting to deal with it, but scientific authorities differ in so many important matters concerning the natural history and migration of the herring, and so little is positively known on the subject, that I think it prudent to avoid controversial points of natural history, and to confine myself to such practical matters as have come under my notice in legislation connected with the Herring Fisheries, and to such improvements for their development as a nautical experience of twelve years in the Navy suggests.

Now the treatment of the subject from the point of view I have indicated, necessitates a reference to statistics. I regret to say that the only reliable figures I can find are those relating to the Scotch Herring Fisheries, compiled by the Fishery Board for Scotland, and I may here remark that I think it is a matter of very great regret that no attention has hitherto been paid to the recommendation of the Sea Fisheries Commission of 1866, who say, "We think it a matter of great importance that Fishery statistics should be systematically collected. It is only by such means that the constant recurrence of the panics to which the Sea Fishery interests have hitherto been subjected can be prevented, and that any trustworthy conclusion can be arrived at regarding the effects of the modes of fishing which are in use. It is probable that the existing Coast Guard or Customs organisation may be utilised to collect statistics, as is now to some extent the case in Ireland."

The necessity for fuller information than we possess concerning our Sea Fisheries must, I feel sure, be impressed on us by the able and interesting paper read on Tuesday by Professor Brown Goode, as the result of the application of improved modes of capture and transit of fish in the United States could not have been established without the elaborate statistics he was able to put before us.

My general observations may be taken as applying to the Herring Fisheries of the United Kingdom, but for the reason I have mentioned they are made with particular reference to what is undoubtedly our most important Herring Fisheries, viz., those of Scotland.

Dealing, in the first instance, with the progress of the

Scotch Herring Fisheries I shall only take you back to the year 1810, when I find by the statistics of the Scotch Fishery Board the number of herrings cured were as follows:

	Barrels cured.	Barrels exported.
1810	90,185	35,848
1830	326,557	181,654
1850	770,698	340,255
1880	1,473,600	1,009,811

I may here mention that a barrel contains 32 gallons English Wine measure, and it is calculated that each barrel contains from 800 to 900 herrings. A barrel of salted herrings, taking the average of the different qualities, represents herrings to the value of 25s. According to this estimate the value of the herrings cured in Scotland in 1880 represents £1,842,000. It is calculated that 20 per cent. of the herrings are sold fresh, assuming the fresh herring to be only worth as much as the cured, although it is probably more valuable, the total quantity taken off the Coast of Scotland in 1880 would represent a money value of £2,210,460.* In the valuable paper prepared for this Conference by the Duke of Edinburgh, His Royal Highness estimates the money value of the fish taken off the Coast of these Islands at £7,380,000. It will thus be seen that the produce of the Scotch Herring Fisheries bears a large proportion to the total value of the fish brought to our shores.

The Herring Fishery of 1880 was the most productive ever experienced in Scotland, and it was one which enabled

---

* Professor Brown Goode estimates the American Oyster Fisheries as producing £2,799,790 a year, £589,330 more than the Scotch Herring Fisheries, the latter being twice as valuable as any other single American Fishery.

the Scotch curer to export a greater quantity of cured herrings to the Continent than either the Norwegians or the Dutch, who have long been the established and worthy rivals of the Scotch in the Continental markets. I find, from the statistics laid before the Herring Brand Committee of 1881, the relative quantity of herrings imported at Stettin was :

	Scotland.	Norway.	Holland.
1869 to 1874, average of 6 years	569,741	936,105	161,961
1875 „ 1880 „ 6 „	629,101	694,502	148,663

The Norwegian barrel is $\frac{1}{6}$th less than the Scotch; the Dutch barrel is the same size.

These figures do not, of course, represent the total export of each country. A quantity of Dutch herrings are sent up the Rhine, and Holland, like Norway and Scotland, has a considerable export trade in cured herrings with most European countries. The Baltic ports, however, take the large proportion of the Scotch and, I believe, also of the Norwegian herrings; a comparison, therefore, of the imports at these ports may be taken as indicating the relative prosperity of the herring trade of the two countries. The demand for cured herrings in the interior of Europe may be shown by a statement of Mr. Reid, the British Vice-Consul at Stettin. Speaking of Scotch herrings imported at Stettin, he said, before the Committee of 1881 : "We send them all round, beginning with Poland and Warsaw and the territory between Stettin and Warsaw, the south of Russia, Gallicia, round by Vienna, along to Bavaria, and then as far round until we get to Magdeburg, when the imports of Hamburgh come in and compete with our offers."

The progress of the Dutch Herring Fisheries is indicated by the statistics in the Exhibition, showing that since 1857 they have increased in value from £47,908 to £147,788 per annum.

Returning to the Scotch Herring Fisheries, I should mention that the herrings cured in 1881 (the last year for which I have reliable statistics) showed a decrease as compared with 1880, of 362,445 barrels, but an increase as compared with the average of the last ten years of 21 per cent.

Besides producing the large revenue I have referred to the Scotch Herring Fisheries give employment to 48,000 fishermen, 2,400 coopers, 18,854 salters and packers. There are 14,800 boats employed, while the value of the boats, nets, and lines is estimated at £1,500,000.

An industry conducted on so large a scale must be of great value to any country. It is difficult to exaggerate its importance to the North of Scotland, where the industries are few, and where the soil is frequently sterile and unproductive.

Professor Huxley in his opening address referred to the large proportion of food frequently taken from the sea as compared with the land. This is well illustrated by the relative products of our Northern Counties.

I once made a calculation, taking my figures from the Domesday Book, that the annual rental of the nine Northern Counties in Scotland, amounted to £1,299,704, being half a million less than the value of the cured herrings in Scotland, already referred to, in 1880, and the value of herrings cured at three stations, in the same year, on the Aberdeenshire Coast, viz.: Aberdeen, Peterhead, and Frazerburgh, exceeded the rental of the County of Aberdeen (the City of Aberdeen alone excepted) by £69,000.

The statistics I have given I think prove the national importance of the Herring Fisheries, they also show that the progress of the Scotch Fisheries, although subject to some slight fluctuations, has been rapid and continuous. I will now consider the conditions under which they have prospered and under which the trade in cured herrings has so greatly increased.

The Herring Fisheries Commission of 1878 reports that up to 1829 it had been the policy of the legislation to encourage the Herring Fisheries by bounties, but the bounties were discontinued, Mr. McCulloch expressing an opinion that the fishermen often went to sea to catch the bounties and not the fish.

From 1829 to 1851 the Fisheries were free from Government sources of encouragement and were subject to no restrictive regulations of importance. From '51 to '67 a series of restrictive measures were passed to regulate the Fishery and to prevent the capture of herrings at certain seasons and in certain ways. Since 1867, again, when the first of the liberating Acts were passed (due in a great degree to the report of the Commission in '62, presided over by my right hon. friend in the chair), the Fisheries on the coast of Scotland have practically been free and subject to no restrictive legislation whatever.

I find that from—

		Average number of barrels cured annually.
1829–51, period of unrestricted fishing	. . .	521,880
1851–68, „ restrictive legislation	. .	657,160
1868–1881, „ unrestricted fishing	. . .	827,580

These figures show that the average increase per annum in 13 years of unrestricted legislation exceeded that of 17 years of restrictive legislation by 170,420 barrels.

The two systems were tried for sufficient periods to justify the conclusion of the Commissioners of '78, viz.— "That legislation in past periods has had no appreciable effect, and that nothing that man has yet done, and nothing man is likely to do, has diminished or is likely to diminish the general stock of herrings in the sea."

If further evidence be needed in support of a policy of unrestricted fishing, it appears to me to be supplied by a consideration of the insignificant proportion of herrings captured by man as compared with that effected by agencies over which man has no control. I need say little on this point, as it was amply dealt with by Professor Huxley in his opening address, but in support of his view I may quote a short extract from the Report of Messrs. Buckland, Walpole and Young in '78. They say: "The Scotch gannets must consume 37 per cent. more herrings than all the Scotch fishermen catch in their nets."

The Commissioners add: "Whales, porpoises, seals, coal fish, predaceous fish of every description are constantly feeding on them (the herrings) from the moment of their birth. The shoals of herrings in the ocean are always accompanied by flocks of gulls and other sea birds, which are continuously preying upon them, and it seems therefore no exaggeration to conclude that man does not destroy one herring for every fifty destroyed by other enemies." In quoting these opinions I am aware that I am only repeating what has frequently been urged before by those who have advocated unrestricted freedom of fishing. My apology for repetition is that I am often being told that "the sea is over-fished," and am frequently appealed to to use my influence in Parliament in support of various restrictive measures for regulating our Sea Fisheries, and the most effective reply to these statements and demands appears to me to be the conclusions arrived at by competent Commissioners, who have made exhaustive inquiries into the subject. Only the other day I read a most interesting book which I purchased in the Exhibition, entitled "The Herring, and the Herring Fisheries," by Mr. de Caux. Mr. de Caux is quite at one with me as to the impracticability of establishing a close time, but he proposes to re-enact the provision contained in the 48th of Geo. III., Chap. 110, regulating the size of the mesh of the herring net. Now this question is very exhaustively dealt with by the Commissioners of 1878. They point out that a law regulating the mesh could not be enforced, except by an International Convention, beyond three miles from the shore. A new Convention has just been concluded with Foreign Powers, and a Bill is now before Parliament to give effect to it, but the Convention declined to entertain the question of the mesh.

Another objection to reducing the size of the mesh is that such a regulation would interfere with the sprat and garvie fishing. I may here assume, without raising any controversial point, that sprats and garvies are not young herrings. Sprats and garvies supply a considerable amount of wholesome food, and it would be unfair to prohibit these fishings on the mere chance of increasing the number of herrings.

A further objection is that the cotton nets, now in universal use, are subject to shrinking at every fresh barking, and fishermen might thus unwittingly be led into an infraction of the law. These difficulties to regulating the size of the mesh, combined with the experience we have had of legislative enactments in Scotland, cause me to differ on this point with Mr. de Caux.

The Act which he desires to pass for the English fisheries is still nominally in force in Scotland, but for the reasons I have stated it has been found to be inoperative, and the newly organized Scotch Fishery Board in their first report, issued last month, recommend the repeal of the section that Mr. de Caux wishes to enforce. They say: "In many cases a net below the standard size is in use; but the fishermen are finding that the small mesh is not profitable, as only the nose of the larger fish gets into it, and unless they get past the gills they are not effectually caught. The matter does not seem to be one suitable for public regulation, and had much better be left to the fishermen themselves. We therefore recommend the repeal of Sec. 12 of 48 Geo. III., Chap. 110."

Legislators received some very wholesome advice from Professor Huxley at the close of his opening address, when he said : "I think that the man who has made the unnecessary law deserves a heavier punishment than the man who breaks it." Now, although some of the laws we have passed to regulate our Herring Fisheries have been harmless, except for bringing the law into contempt, yet this cannot be said of all our restrictive legislation, as the Sea Fisheries Commission of '66 describes the effect of the close time established by Parliament on the West Coast of Scotland, as "reducing the population of some of the Western Islands to misery and starvation, while abundant food was lying in front of their doors, by preventing them taking herrings." Surely Parliament can be better employed than by mischievous legislation, producing such vexatious results.

The statistics I have quoted indicate the general prosperity of the Scotch Herring Fisheries, but this general conclusion must be accepted with some qualification. The Commissioners of 1878 remark that the so-called prosperity is almost entirely due to the extraordinary development of the fisheries off the Aberdeenshire coast ; and if the takes between Fraserburgh and Montrose be deducted, the condition of the other fisheries will be found to be much less satisfactory. Commenting on this, the Commissioners observe that the development of the fisheries on the Aberdeenshire coast has led to the neglect of fisheries at other places, the younger and more vigorous fishermen being attracted to the most productive fishing ground. The destruction of the Wick Harbour has caused many of the boats from that district to fish off the Aberdeenshire coast.

These causes have contributed to the falling off of the fisheries elsewhere. But allowing for these considerations, the Commissioners express an opinion that the vast amount of netting now in use may have scared the fish from narrow waters. They estimate the nets used by the Scotch herring fishers to be sufficient to reach in a continuous line for 12,000 miles, to cover an area of 70 square miles, and to be sufficient to go three times across the Atlantic from Liverpool to New York. The substitution of cotton for hemp nets may be said to have revolutionised the fishery. A boat that used to carry 960 yards of netting, now carries 3,300 yards. The nets used to be 6 or 7 yards, they are now 10 yards deep. They used to present a catching surface of 3,000 square yards, they now present a catching surface of 33,000 square yards; without increasing the weight of the nets to be worked, each boat has increased its catching power fivefold. This vast extent of netting certainly warrants the possibility assumed by the Commissioners, that the nets may have scared the herrings from narrow waters, but looking to the general results, they decline to recommend any restrictive measures, entertaining an opinion that the vast amount of netting has no effect in diminishing the stock of herrings in the sea; a conclusion amply justified by the enormous take of herrings in 1880, two years after the Commissioners' Report. Since then herrings have also returned in greater number to some of our inshore fisheries. Referring to the west coast, the Fishery Board Report for 1881 mentions that "The best fishing was got in Loch Hourn, where an immense body of herrings remained all the season." It is reasonable to assume that the herrings returned on their own account, and that their movements were made in "blissful ignorance" that the British Parliament had abolished the measures for their special protection.

Another feature of the Scotch Herring Fisheries is the large and continually increasing takes of late years off the Shetland Islands. In 1879 the Shetlanders only cured 8,000 barrels; in 1880 the number had increased to 48,000; in 1881 to 59,586, and in 1882 to 134,000 barrels.

In his opening address Professor Huxley remarked that considering the antiquity and importance of the fishing industry "it is singular that it can hardly be said to have kept pace with the rapid improvement of almost every other branch of industrial occupation in modern times. If we contrast the progress of fishery with that of agriculture, for example, the comparison is not favourable to fishery," and he afterwards observed, "But we are still very far behind scientific agriculture; and as to the application of machinery and of steam to fishery operations, it may be said that in this country a commencement has been made, but hardly more."

I am not going to question the general accuracy of Professor Huxley's conclusions, yet I think that I have shown that our Scotch Herring Fisheries have not been altogether standing still. The increase in our take of herrings has not been entirely due to the larger amount of capital invested in the trade, nor to the enterprise of our fishermen in going further to sea in pursuit of their calling; though no doubt these two causes have largely contributed in raising our fishery to its present importance. But of late years the boats have been very much improved, and the cotton nets, as I have already said, worked almost a revolution in the Herring Fisheries. The effect of these combined causes, better boats and better nets, will at once be appreciated by a reference to a table compiled by Mr. Francis Day (from the Scotch Fishery Board statistics), and published in his notes, giving an account of his cruise in the *Triton* last year.

Mr. Day gives the proportion of barrels of cured herrings to the fishermen employed since 1825 :—

	Fishermen.	Barrels.
5 years, 1825–30	1	8
5 „ 1854–59	1	14
5 „ 1876–81	1	22

One fisherman now produces nearly three times what he did fifty years ago, and the result of his labour will bear favourable comparison with the increased production of the agricultural labourers during that period. I am, however, quite at one with Professor Huxley in believing that our sea fisheries are capable of far greater development, particularly by the application of steam power. On this point, I may be permitted to quote some opinions I expressed in a lecture I gave about two years ago, when I advocated the application of steam power as a means of developing our Herring Fisheries.

What I claim for steam is :—

    1. A saving of life by increasing the boat's chance of making a port of safety in bad weather.

    2. A certainty of reaching and returning from the fishing ground in all ordinary weather, independent of tides, calms, and head winds.

    3. The comparative punctuality thus acquired by

steam would enable arrangements to be made by railways to run fish trains, and so enhance the value of the cargo by the difference between the price of fresh and cured fish.

In the foregoing remarks I have assumed that each boat should be propelled by steam power—an auxiliary screw would be the most suitable. Steam might also be applied to a winch, and would save a deal of manual labour in hauling the nets. Steam tugs, to tow the boats, have been tried with only a moderate degree of success. As a means of saving life by getting the boats into harbour in a storm they are not to be depended on, and at any time might miss the boats during a fog or in a dark night. Steam carriers do not appear to me to be adapted for the herring fisheries. The transhipment of herrings from the present boats to carriers, except in very smooth water, would be attended with great difficulty. How steam can be best utilised in developing our herring fisheries is a question I should be very glad to hear discussed at this Conference. It is one of great and growing importance.

Our first-class boats, annually in some parts of Scotland going further to sea, are too heavy to be propelled by oars; consequently, in calms or when a tide has to be encountered, the cargo of herrings is frequently spoilt before it reaches the shore. The regulations of the new Fishery Board are framed to facilitate the curing of herrings at sea, but our present boats are not large enough to carry barrels and salt enough for this purpose. Off the coast of Montrose, where I believe our boats often go seventy to eighty miles to sea, I am told that it is now the practice to carry salt enough to sprinkle over the herrings, and thus save them for four or five days; and I understand that herrings treated in this method, termed "salting in bulk," are but slightly depreciated in the market; but herrings so cured would not be entitled to receive the Government "brand" or mark, the regulation for this purpose requiring that the fish should be cured within twenty-four hours of being caught.

The Government brand, indicating a degree of quality, was first established in 1808, but nothing was charged for it till 1859, when the Government imposed a fee of 4*d.* a barrel to defray the cost of the branding establishment. The amount collected from the fees exceeds the cost of branding by about £3,000 a year, and this surplus is now paid to the Scotch Fishery Board for harbour improvements and other objects to develop the fisheries.

The policy of a Government brand has been the subject of frequent contention among the Scotch curers. The matter was fully discussed so recently before a parliamentary Committee, of which I had the honour to be chairman, that I do not propose to detain you to-day by reopening the question.

The Committee referred to reported in 1881 in favour of the retention of the brand. It was contended by its opponents that the brand had lost its value, but the Committee considered "the continental merchants would not continue to demand branded herrings, and the home curer would not voluntarily pay 4*d.* a barrel for a trade mark which had ceased to be a guarantee of quality." I should mention that the brand is not compulsory; and if any of the Scotch curers consider they can establish a superior trade mark—and some of them are of opinion that they can—they are at perfect liberty to do so.

The Dutch cure most of their herrings at sea, on board much larger vessels than are generally used by our fishermen, but I should regret to see the adoption of a system here by which the fish offal was all lost, as it forms an excellent manure, which, by a process shown in the Exhibition, might, I believe, be made still more valuable. The result of the experience obtained at the Menhaden Fishery, detailed by Professor Brown Goode, is instructive, as showing the extent to which fish offal may be advantageously utilised.*

The use of larger boats necessitates increased harbour accommodation, and this is at present the great want of fishermen all along our coast. How it is to be supplied is too large a question for me fully to discuss in this Paper. There can be no doubt, especially after the experience we have had in this Exhibition, of the demand on the part of the public for an abundant supply of cheap fresh fish; I am not, however, aware to what extent the community is willing to be taxed for the construction of better harbours to facilitate a supply of food so universally appreciated, but without better harbours I believe it will be impossible for

[1] " In 1878 the Menhaden Oil and Guano Industry employed capital to the amount of 2,350,000 dollars, 3,337 men, 64 steamers, 279 sailing vessels, and consumed 777,000,000 of fish. There were 56 factories, which produced 1,392,644 gallons of oil, valued at 450,000 dollars, and 55,154 tons of crude guano, valued at 600,000 dollars; this was a poor year. In 1874, the number of gallons produced was 3,373,000; in 1875, 2,681,000; in 1876, 2,992,000; in 1877, 2,427,000. In 1878, the total value of manufactured products was 1,050,000 dollars; in 1874, this was 1,809,000 dollars; in 1875, 1,582,000 dollars; in 1876, 1,671,000 dollars; in 1877, 1,608,000 dollars; it should be stated that in these reports only four-fifths of the whole number of factories are included. The refuse of the oil factory supplies a material of much value for manures. As a base for nitrogen it enters largely into the composition of most of the manufactured fertilisers. The amount of nitrogen derived from this source in 1875 was estimated to be equivalent to that contained in 60,000,000 lbs. of Peruvian guano, the gold value of which would not have been far from 1,920,000 dollars."—*Professor Brown Goode's Paper at International Fisheries Exhibition.*

the fishermen to meet the growing demands of an increasing population. State aid towards harbour improvement has hitherto been most successful, when given in the form of grants to supplement local efforts, or by loan at a low rate of interest. Under this system, which I should like to see extended, such harbours, and they are miserably inadequate, as are available for our Herring Fisheries, have been mainly constructed. In Scotland generally, the fishermen have shown a commendable spirit of self-reliance by combining together to raise funds for the improvement of their harbours. I have often been astonished at the efforts they have made to enable them to participate in the small grant annually given to the Scotch Fishery Board.

I may mention one instance that lately came under my notice. About two years ago I was visiting a small fishing hamlet on the coast of Banffshire. I was told that the fishermen were most anxious to raise a sum of £3,000, to enable them, by the assistance of the Fishery Board, to improve their harbour. I remarked to a friend who was with me, that there seemed to be nobody but fishermen in the place, and I expressed some doubt as to their ability to raise the required sum. His reply entirely confirmed my estimate of the inhabitants, for he said, "No one here puts on a black coat on the Sabbath except the minister and the general merchant." Yet the amount required, with some assistance from the landlord, was duly raised, and by the aid of the Fishery Board a harbour, which will be of great advantage to the district, is now being constructed. I mention this circumstance because I think the willingness of the fishermen to pay, so far as in their power, for improved harbours, is a consideration which should be taken into account in any general scheme for harbour construction, and also because I think the spirit of self-reliance evinced by the fishermen entitles them to the sympathy and to the support of the public.

I should like to say a word before concluding this Paper on the distribution of the vast number of herrings taken off the Scotch coast. The Duke of Edinburgh estimates the value of the fish taken by the trawlers off the coast of the United Kingdom at £2,581,000, or about £300,000 more than the value of the herrings taken off the Scotch coast. Cured herrings, representing £1,006,462, were exported in 1881, the value of the other fish exported that year from all parts of the kingdom was only £398,048. It will thus be seen that the distribution of the herrings is very different from that of other fish. I believe a far greater proportion of the Scotch herrings, especially those caught on the west coast, would be consumed as fresh fish at home, if greater facilities were given by the railways for their conveyances.*

The evidence given before the Railway Committee last year, fully exposes the high rates frequently imposed by

---

[1] "Still more important has been the general adoption of scientific methods of preparation and transportation. Great freezing houses have been built on the Great Lakes, on the Pacific coast, and in the cities of the East, and refrigerator cars are running upon all the trunk lines of railway. Columbia salmon, lake white-fish, cod, bass, Spanish mackerel, and other choice fishes are frozen stiff and packed up in heaps like cordwood, and can be had at any season of the year. Refrigerator cars carry unfrozen fish from sea and lake inland. Smelts and trout, packed in snow in the north, are received in New York by the cartload daily throughout the winter. Halibut are brought from the distant oceanic banks in refrigerators built in the holds of the vessels, and 12,000,000 to 14,000,000 pounds are distributed, packed in ice, to the cities of the interior. Baltimore, from September to April, sends special trains laden with oysters, daily, into the west, and Chesapeake oysters are food for all, not luxuries, even beyond the Mississippi."—*Professor Brown Goode.*

the railway companies for the carriage of fresh fish. A less grasping policy would, I believe, be more remunerative to the railways and certainly more advantageous to the public. But this is a subject which will be more fully discussed in a subsequent Paper by his Excellency Mr. Spencer Walpole.

The conclusion I arrive at is, that the requirements for the further development of our herring fisheries are :—

1. Better harbour accommodation.
2. The application of steam power.
3. Increased railway facilities, and lower railway rates for the distribution of fresh fish.

As my right hon. friend Mr. Shaw-Lefevre, M.P., is to read a Paper on the " Principles of Legislation in connection with Sea Fisheries," I have not alluded to the laws relating to trawling, and other matters for regulating our sea fisheries ; I have only touched on a subject, which I am sure will be more ably dealt with by my right hon. friend, to such an extent as I deemed necessary to make the condition of our herring fisheries intelligible before an International Conference.

Regarding the objects in the Exhibition calculated to develope the herring fisheries, there are models of boats of the most approved build propelled both by steam and sail, nets of the most improved pattern, conspicuously among them being the American purse-seine net, admirably adapted, in the opinion of some competent practical men with whom I inspected it, for the herring fisheries ; there are refrigerating vans, and barrels made by steam machinery.

But more important to my mind than the modern appliances I have referred to for the capture and transit of fish are the conclusions arrived at by the competent authorities who have addressed us at the Conference, viz., that the stock of herrings in the sea, so far as man is concerned, is practically inexhaustible. The opinion expressed by the Playfair Commission in '62, by the Sea Fisheries Commission in '66, by the Herring Fisheries Commission in '78, is confirmed by the exhaustive enquiries of the Duke of Edinburgh, and by the ripe experience of Professor Huxley. Although we cannot account for the mysterious movements of the herring, causing the fluctuation which characterise our fishery, it is at least some consolation to know on the high authorities I have mentioned, that although advancing civilisation may pollute our rivers and destroy our salmon, we are still likely to enjoy our herring, as the inventive genius of the age has failed to discover any means of depriving us of an ample supply of the most abundant and nutritious food which the bounty of the ocean yields to the labour of man.

DISCUSSION.

The CHAIRMAN said his honourable friend had treated the subject as he had expected he would from the intelligent action which he had taken in Parliament in promoting regulating but not restrictive laws, with regard to sea fisheries. The only reason he presumed why he found himself in the Chair on this occasion was, that in 1862 he was Chairman of the Royal Commission for examining into the herring-fisheries of the British coast. Why he, a Chemical Professor, should be found in that position, he could never fully understand, especially as there was on the Commission a man of European eminence, and of the greatest authority on fisheries: though they both were in the same galley, and he sat at the helm, it was the vigorous power of his friend, Professor Huxley, who not only impelled the bark, but also directed it. That Commission established one or two facts which certainly had been of the greatest importance to our great fisheries, viz., that restrictive laws framed by man in ignorance of the laws of Nature, were excessively destructive to the interests of fishermen instead of being favourable to them. When they first began to examine this subject, they found different laws prevailing on the east coast of Scotland to those which prevailed on the west. On the east coast there were no restrictive laws, and fishermen were encouraged to catch fish, even full fish containing ova, in order to be cured. Each of these fish had on an average 50,000 eggs, and the enormous number that were taken in this state would seem to indicate a process of extermination; but the fisheries of the east coast, without restrictive laws, increased, and did not diminish. When they went to the west coast of Scotland, however, in the inner waters of the Firth of Clyde, they found restrictive laws prevailing. For several months no herrings were allowed to be taken, there being a close time for herrings for the purpose of protecting them. As they went further into the open waters at the Firth of Forth and Clyde along the islands up to near the Highlands, those restrictive laws still prevailed; but there was a relaxation as to the period when the close time should end. A very curious result was made apparent, and a most unexpected one. At the periods of close time, the herrings came to the banks to spawn, and were followed by their natural enemies in great number, among which he might chiefly allude to the cod and the ling, which consumed them in great numbers. There were innumerable fish which lived upon the young fry and the full-grown herring; the cod, ling, dog-fish, and conger, fed on the full-grown herring; while the flat-fish and crabs eat the spawn, and there were innumerable other fish which eat herring-fry. At the time when they found them on their spawning banks, these fish had an appetite for nothing else but herring, and this result followed, that the fishermen of cod and ling could catch nothing, because they would only take herring bait at the time, and the close time prevented the fishermen getting any herring-bait for catching this white fish. The consequence was, that the laws invented for the protection of the herring became laws for their destruction, because their natural enemies, which could not be caught because of the want of bait, multiplied exceedingly, and devoured the very herrings which the laws intended to protect. This was so to an enormous extent, as a little calculation would show. The Commission frequently opened cod and ling and examined the contents of their stomachs, in which they frequently found seven to ten herrings, which they had not begun to digest; but allowing a diet of two herrings a day to a cod, and allowing him to live seven months in one year, fifty cod would catch as many herrings as one fisherman could catch in a year. Now there was no census of how many cod and ling existed, but there was a census of how many cod and ling were caught; there were caught and salted last year on the coast of Scotland, 115,513 cwt. of cod and ling. Now about thirty fish went to a hundredweight, and from a little calculation it would follow, that if the cod and ling which were salted had lived in the sea, and had not been taken, they would have caught as many herrings as 69,000 fishermen. Now that was more than 20,000 beyond all the fishermen who existed on those coasts, and, therefore, those laws which protected the enemies of herrings, kept them in the sea, and produced this enormous loss. That was one of the results of the Commission; for the laws intended for the protection of herring really multiplied the natural enemies of the herrings enormously, and thus destroyed them infinitely more than they were protected. The action of that was this, that under the protection of these laws, the fish which preyed on the herring increased and multiplied exceedingly, so that they had a very good time; but the poor fishermen of those coasts had a very bad time, because they could not catch the fish upon which their subsistence depended. The consequence was, that they found these fishermen disobeying the law, when it could not be enforced, or when the law was obeyed, it led to starvation, and they were obliged to emigrate. That was the result of interfering with the laws of nature by an indiscreet law passed by Parliament. The lesson which might be drawn from the interesting paper just read, was that though Parliament might make laws for keeping order and safety amongst fishermen; that the balance of nature which prevailed in the sea should be left alone, because the balance of animal life depended upon unknown factors. The herrings had for their food small crustaceæ, sometimes microscopic, but at other times little shrimps and sand-eels. They enjoyed that food, and when it existed on the coast, multiplied largely; but whilst they lived on these things, there were other fish which were living on them, and which had the greatest love for the herrings. They were the conger, the dog-fish, the cod, and the ling, which slew their millions, and there were birds, such as gulls and gannets, which also destroyed multitudes, and then there were the porpoises and grampuses, which ate up whole shoals of herrings. This was the balance of life, one balancing the other, and the more it was interfered with, the more mischief resulted. Sometimes there was a cry for protective laws, because the herring fishery varied as any other industry varied according to circumstances. They did not always know why it varied. For instance, Mr. Duff spoke about the varying character of the herring, and a very capricious fish was the usual term fishermen applied to it. But the term caprice was merely the mode of concealing our ignorance of its habits. If we knew its habits, and those of its enemies, it would probably be found there was no caprice in the matter. Sometimes herrings came in shoals to particular parts of the coast, and other times they abandoned them for many years. The reason of that was not known. It might be, for instance, that something had happened to the small crustaceæ and the sand-eels on the particular part of the coast, and the herrings did not find their natural food; it might be that the enemies of the herrings had multiplied very much, and devoured in too large quantities their own subsistences. Then the herrings decreased, but ultimately they increased again, because their enemies having fed too largely upon them, they decreased in number, and then the herrings had their turn again, and so there was a continual scarcity and plenty in the markets, sometimes prosperity and sometimes a panic, and the herring in its action assisted in producing these cases of prosperity and panic, just as if they were Lancashire manufacturers. It was needless, therefore, to make laws to try and prevent man, who was such a very small factor in the result, catching herrings when there were, all round the herrings, enemies creating havoc infinitely greater. If any lesson could be learnt from the interesting paper they had listened to, it was that it would be much better to leave these things to the laws of nature, which were far more wise in this respect than any laws which were likely to be passed by Parliament.

Dr. FRANCIS DAY did not know whether it was worth while making many remarks on the question if they were told that all legislation was useless, and that whoever said anything on the other side appeared to be one who did not understand the subject upon which he was speaking; but he thought they were met for the purpose of discussion, to hear both sides of the question, and not to jump to conclusions at the commencement before they had heard what the other side had to say. Personally as yet he gave no opinion on one side or the other, but he did think those who had opinions to offer should be allowed to give them without being told that those who made laws ought to suffer from them themselves instead of the unfortunate fishermen to whom those laws would apply. He could not help thinking that gentlemen who held those views, though they might be very fit for Legislatures, were quite unfit to legislate on fishing matters. It was only necessary to look at the fresh-water fisheries to see how they had been destroyed for want of legislation, and what had been done by making use of legislation. He would, however, pass on to the subject more immediately before them; he had no intention of making any remarks when he entered the hall, but he had been at two or three conferences when no one had risen to say anything, except the proposers and seconders of resolutions, and he thought it was time that a few observations should be made on the different sides of these important questions. They must all feel exceedingly obliged to Mr. Duff for the figures he had given, but when he left out the natural history of the subject it appeared to him that he left out the most important portion of the question with regard to herring and other fisheries. There were three different classes of fish from the sea which were mostly made use of by man. There were the herrings, the gregarious form, which were mostly found near the surface, and with them might be classed the mackerel and the pilchard, and then there were the deep sea form of the cod and ling which had been mentioned, the devourers of the herring, and also the ground fishes, such as the turbot, sole, &c. Some people talked about the balance of nature, and said no law should be passed with reference to these fisheries, but the question was whether by passing no laws they were not destroying the balance of nature. They permitted the cod and these voracious fishes to be captured in large quantities, and these were the very fish which, as the Chairman informed them, ate the herring. Might it not be that if, as many fishermen told them (though it was denied on some hands, as far as he had seen, it appeared to be correct), the inshore fisheries were decreasing, the quantity of cod was decreased, and so the fish were destroyed which were catching the herring, and thus the herring might be increasing in consequence of the destruction of the cod fisheries. Then they were told that in consequence of the legislation the poor fishermen suffered on one portion of the coast of Scotland and not on the other, but if they turned to the blue book issued by Messrs. Buckland and Walpole it would be found that although these regulations were in existence they were never carried out; that no regulations ever passed by man had ever had any effect on the herring fisheries. Then they were told that the herrings were inexhaustible. They found the herrings migrating from place to place, and in so doing they disappeared entirely from one country and appeared in another. If the cod fisheries were destroyed and the herrings migrated, where would the fisheries be? He had seen the oil sardine on the western coast of India for years, and all of a sudden it would entirely disappear and not appear again for several seasons. With regard to the size of the mesh he would not attempt to offer any opinion, seeing there were so many gentlemen present more competent to speak upon it. It appeared to him that if the herrings were driven out from the inshore fisheries into the open sea there was a necessity for larger boats, and if this resulted, and there was not an increase of harbour accommodation, what were the fishermen to do on the eastern coast of Scotland? They must be driven down to the ports or beach their boats, which often caused loss of life. He thought, instead of taking all the facts given in these Royal Commissions for granted, they ought to have them supplemented by further investigation. If investigations were carried on in the way in which they were in the United States, so as to ascertain whether any class of fish were increasing or decreasing, what they fed upon, and what it was which caused their food to increase or decrease, or to migrate, they would then be in a better position to judge as to the necessity for legislation on this subject.

Mr. BRADY (Inspector of Irish Fisheries) said he had listened with great pleasure to the excellent address which had been given, and it was certainly a question of very deep interest whether, as we went on increasing our means of capture, and increasing the amount of food brought up from the ocean, we might not be considered to be killing the goose which laid the golden eggs. He had had the honour on two occasions of mentioning certain facts connected with two bays in Ireland, from which he drew certain conclusions, which, of course, might be incorrect, but those conclusions were that all restrictions on deep-sea fishing were mischievous, and tended to no good. If he understood aright the observations of the last speaker, he said the regulations in Scotland had no effect on the herring fishery. There had been restrictions, and the Chairman had made some very important observations with regard to them. Dr. Day said they were not enforced, and, therefore, they had no effect. Well, if they found the herring fisheries of Scotland increased in the vast proportions that they had done for so many years, it was the strongest argument that the restrictions placed upon them by the Legislature were of no avail, and did no good. How far, if they had been enforced, they might have done any good, of course no one could say. It was most important that science should be brought to bear on this question, and should be aided by practical experience. When they had arrived at the time when scientific men could say that certain restrictions should be placed on deep-sea fishing, then it would be time for the Legislature to step in, but until that day came it would be only mischievous to cripple the industry of a country by imposing such restrictions in the absence of that knowledge which they all admitted they were deficient in. The great deficiency of statistics had been referred to especially with regard to Ireland, and he regretted very much to say that the statistics of fisheries in Ireland were miserably defective. It was very important that those statistics should be collected, so that they might ascertain whether the improved modes of capture and the greater distance to which the boats went were injurious to the fisheries. Nothing was more interesting to him than something which he had seen in the Exhibition, which might develop the fisheries to an enormous extent. He alluded to a mode adopted on the great lakes in Canada, by which a steamer while moving on, kept paying out one net, and at the same time hauled in another. If that could be brought into operation in our sea fisheries it would lead to very important changes.

Mr. McLELAN (Canada), said that some of the fishing grounds on the great lakes in Canada, where the mode of fishing just referred to was adopted, were 400 or 500 miles long; and the reports coming from fishermen were, that unrestricted fishing diminished the number of fish even in these large lakes. Application had been made to him repeatedly to permit a smaller sized mesh of net to be used; but in consequence of the testimony which had come to him from all fishermen, he had refused to allow it. He considered it was a very important question whether sea fisheries were exhaustible or not; probably the most important question which could be discussed. Previous to coming to England, all the testimony he had received from the fishermen of Canada, both shore fishermen and sea fishermen, was, that on the great lakes, fisheries that had hitherto been very profitable, were being exhausted from over-fishing, and from all he could hear from fishermen all round the coast, he had come to the conclusion that it was possible to exhaust the fisheries of the Dominion of Canada. Mr. Duff had told them that with regard to herrings they first had an open season, in which an average of 500,000 barrels of fish were taken every year; then for some seventeen years they had a close season, in which there was an average of 600,000 barrels, and then it was made open again, and the average rose to 800,000 barrels. The inference from all this was, that it was better to have free fishing; but at the same time the honourable gentleman stated that the appliances for catching the herrings had been multiplied fivefold, and it occurred to him that if that were so, they ought to have had three million barrels of fish instead of 800,000, seeing the appliances had so largely increased. Then the question arose, with these multiplied appliances and the improved boats which had been referred to, was it not the fact that they went further to sea, and were sweeping over a larger area and not getting a proportionate return of fish? This was a point on which the testimony of practical men was needed. Science told them that fish produced so many eggs, and multiplied very fast; that one fish fed on another; and that the balance of nature ought to be preserved; that the little fish had larger fish to eat them; the larger fish had bigger ones to bite them, and so on *ad infinitum;* but they left out of sight a certain kind of fish which preyed on the others, but were not fit for food and therefore were not caught. To keep up the balance of nature they ought to fit out expeditions to destroy those fish which preyed on the edible fish; but if they left them to multiply and prey on the others, and at the same time man went in with his fivefold machines to catch the herrings, the result would be, according to the testimony of Canada, that the fishing grounds would be gradually destroyed. It would simplify things on the other side of the Atlantic very much if it could be settled, by the testimony of fishermen and the investigations of science, that the sea fisheries were inexhaustible; then all they would have to do would be to improve their appliances for catching. Mr. Duff had referred to the want of harbours round the coast, and if he might be permitted to give the experience of a young country, he might say that they had felt the same want in Canada; but there the Government took hold of the matter, considering it of great public importance that the fisheries of the country should be protected, and that suitable harbours should be provided. Year by year large grants were made for the erection of suitable breakwaters and harbours of refuge, with the most beneficial results. He did not pretend to argue the advisability of this system in a country where it was the State policy for every industry to be left to its own resources; but in Canada, which might be considered more protective of native industries, that course had been pursued, and fishermen had been protected not only by the providing of harbours, but by the distribution yearly of a quarter of a million of dollars in the encouragement of fisheries.

Mr. RONALD MACDONALD (Aberdeen), said the views of gentlemen from England, Ireland, and Canada had been heard, and as he came from Scotland, where the herring fisheries were more important than in either England or Ireland, he hoped he might be allowed to make a few remarks. He knew a number of Mr. Duff's constituents, who appreciated very much the great intelligence and practical interest he had taken in the development of fishing in Scotland, and he had listened with great pleasure to the comprehensive paper which he had read; but it could not be expected that everything which might be supposed to be even of essential importance to the subject, could be compressed into so short a paper. On one point there seemed to be a little want of unanimity, namely, the uselessness or otherwise of legislation with regard to fisheries. The views on this subject came from two different quarters, and they differed according to the quarter from which they came. Some years ago he had the opportunity of being present when evidence was laid before the Commission which had been referred to, when Mr. Buckland, Mr. Walpole, and Mr. Young went round on the east and west coasts of Scotland, and he found that all those who were interested in the inshore fishing demanded that there should be restrictions, while those who depended on the system of fishing which was now so successful, namely, employing bigger boats, bigger nets, more of them, and going out sixty, seventy, or a hundred miles to sea, and catching the herrings before they came into the small bays, these came to the conclusion that it was practically useless, if not mischievous, to make such laws as those who had little boats and depended on fishing in 'the small inland lakes demanded. He was not prepared to say that the gentlemen from Canada were wrong in saying that it would be perhaps dangerous to do away with restrictions there; but it must be borne in mind, that large as the Canadian lakes were, they were different from the Atlantic ocean, and whilst restrictions in Canada might be useful, it did not follow that such restrictions would be of any use when dealing with such a large space of water as the Atlantic. There was just one omission in Mr. Duff's comprehensive paper which he should like to bring under the notice of the many eminent men whom he was glad to see were taking a practical interest in this matter. Hardly any reference was made to the fishing on the west coast of Scotland, a comparatively new enterprise, which was carried on in the open sea. There had been for many years from 1,000 to 2,000 boats engaged in that way, not in the Loch Earne, not in the Firth of Clyde, but out from the outer Hebrides into the Atlantic. They began to get fish there on the 24th of May, and continued up to the present time, and a very large quantity was caught there. The facilities for sending it to market, however, were very bad indeed. One fact would show the extent of that fishing industry. In a Parliamentary paper submitted to the House of Commons not long ago, it appeared that from the railway station at Oban, three times as much fish was despatched as from any other station. Upwards of 12,000 tons of herrings were sent from that station, whilst the total quantity sent on the whole Caledonian railway system, including all the towns from Aberdeen to Montrose, was only about 25,000 tons. He hoped, therefore, that some account would be taken of this newly developed fishery out in the Atlantic, by boats coming from Montrose, Fraserburgh, and all the north-eastern points to Stornoway. There was no telegraphic communication of any kind, and the people were put to a very great inconvenience in consequence of having no facilities for sending their fish to market, or getting salt or anything else when they had a large supply of fish.

Mr. JOHNSON (Montrose) said he was one of the jury to examine the salmon nets and fixed nets, and whilst examining these nets he had been very much interested in the exhibits from foreign countries. For many years they had been fishing with the same nets with very little improvement except, as Mr. Duff had said, that they had substituted cotton for hemp, and had made, what they called in Scotland "clipper nets." The first thing which the jury discussed was the steamer on the Canadian lakes, which had been already referred to. It was the first thing which took his attention and had riveted it ever since, and he had wondered whether it could be adapted for herring fishing. It could be seen in the Canadian department, and was shooting a net over the stern and was hauling one in at the bow at the same time. He did not expect that that would ever be carried out in the herring fishery, but he thought it came nearest to anything he had ever seen for doing what appeared very desirable, viz., having some mechanical means of reeling up the nets. The only difficulty which he saw in the way was in reeling up the herring nets to get clear of the buoys that buoyed it up. So impressed was he with the adaptability of that steamer that he was quite prepared, with the sanction of the Executive Committee, on behalf of his firm in Montrose, to offer a prize to any one who should adopt that system and make it workable for the east coast herring fishery. The next thing he noticed was the purse seine. He understood that was largely used in America, and he thought if it were brought into use in the herring fishery it would revolutionise the trade to a large extent. If they could get these nets to work on these large steamers they could soon bring them into port. For some years past when the boats had been going longer distances, instead of coming in in twenty-four hours they were sometimes three days; and he recollected on one Sunday morning about £500 worth of herrings had to be carted direct to the manure heap because they had been three days in the boat instead of one. He should also be glad to give a premium in connection with the purse seine if it could be made available for herring fishing. The only other matter he would speak about was a cod net which was entirely new to him but which was exhibited in the Norwegian, Swedish, and Canadian sections. The nets of Norway and Sweden were what would be called gill nets, or hung nets, sinking to the bottom. He had never heard of a cod in Scotland or England being caught in any net except the trawl. He should like, if possible, to bring these three nets and the steamer before the fishermen of the United Kingdom, and would suggest that it would be very valuable if some of the illustrated newspapers would give drawings of the net and as much explanation about them as their friends from those countries would be willing to impart.

Mr. WILMOT (Canadian Commissioner), having heard the Canadian name mentioned conspicuously in regard to a particular description of net, wished to say a word upon it. He was not going to discuss the question of herring fisheries to any great extent, but merely to state, as he did on a former occasion, that if herrings were caught in such vast numbers as it was proposed to do by these machines it must more or less affect all other fish inshore. The herring was the principal food of a large class of fish, and if they were destroyed to such an extent by these improved machines and all the ingenuity which man could bring to bear, not only would the herring be exterminated, but it would very seriously affect the other fish which fed upon them. He regretted very much to find that the system pursued in Canada was now being taken hold of so readily by gentlemen from Scotland for the destruction of these poor innocent fish. These things were sent over merely to illustrate the mode by which fish were sometimes caught in Canada, and it was being taken hold of to exterminate, to a greater extent than was now done, the class of fish which in Canada they were desirous of protecting. The herring of Canada was a different fish from the herring of the sea; it was a salmonoid very much superior to the herring of the sea, and at one time existed in vast abundance in the inland lakes of Canada. In some of those lakes there were now no herrings left at all, and the consequence was there were no salmon, no salmon trout, and none of the many species of fish which feed on those herrings. If this could be done in a short period of time in the great inland seas of Canada, the same results would follow here if these destructive engines were adopted, and no protection given to the fish. The food of the larger fish must not be destroyed if they were to be retained. The Almighty had made all things wisely; He caused the herring to multiply beyond almost any other fish, because it was fed upon more largely than any other description, consequently the herring must produce a greater number to keep up their kind, and if they went on inventing engines, and using every effort to destroy the smaller fish simply because he was small, the result would be to exterminate the larger ones. However he would not speak at any length on this subject, because he anticipated it would come up for discussion later. He rose to thank his friends who had thought proper to draw attention to the superior modes of fishing to a certain extent pursued in Canada, and to warn them not to use it very largely, for fear that if they did, they would destroy the vast supplies of herrings in the sea, and as a consequence the larger and better description of fish also.

Earl DUCIE then proposed a vote of thanks to Mr. Duff for the paper he had read, which was very valuable, not only in itself, but for having produced what one of the speakers had called a want of unanimity, which he considered to be one of the most valuable features of the discussion. Mr. Duff had treated of the history of the herring during the present century, but he remembered in the course of the discussion that he had read in Gibbon, who, when treating of one of the early eruptions of the barbarians in the early Christian ages, and describing the effects that it had on Europe, told them that it had even interfered with the herring trade on the coast of the North Sea, and he would commend that remark to the investigation of anybody who proposed to write the history of the herring.

Sir GEORGE CAMPBELL seconded the motion. He said in these days of division of labour, however talented a man might be, he never was so effective as he might be, unless he devoted himself specially to one subject. That was what his friend Mr. Duff had done, and he had done so with good effect. He showed, in his own person, that a good sailor and a good fisherman was likely to make a good member of Her Majesty's Government, and so he was heartily welcomed in the function which he fulfilled in the

House of Commons. He had not only given a deal of useful information, but had given rise to a very interesting discussion. These were days in which Radicals were found attacking our oldest institutions; next to the Bible, he thought nothing was so firmly fixed on the Englishman as the old proverb that there were as good fish in the sea as ever came out of it, but even that had been questioned to-day, and had led to a very lively discussion. He did not pretend to say which side was right; he would only observe, as another speaker had done, that there might be two sides to this question, as regarded the deep sea and the inland waters. His attention was especially called to that from the observation of Mr. Wilmot, from which it appeared that the American herring was totally different from our herrings; but the discussion had been with regard to the European herring, and he thought there was a great deal of weight in the arguments and the facts stated by Mr. Duff.

The motion having been passed unanimously,

Mr. DUFF, M.P., in reply, said he had been very glad to have aroused such an interesting discussion. He would not enter into the question at any length, but he might be permitted to recall to the recollection of the audience a distinction drawn by Professor Huxley in his opening address. He said there were two kinds of fishing, fresh-water fishing and salt-water fishing, and while it could be shown that you could over-fish and destroy fish in fresh water, there was nothing to prove that salt-water fish were exhaustible. This had a bearing on the remarks made by Mr. MacLelan and Mr. Wilmot, because both those gentlemen's observations had reference to the fresh-water fishing and the lake fishing. Dr. Day, who spoke of sea fisheries, did not quite go the length of saying what they were to do. He rather criticised his observations, without putting forward any alternative scheme. He did not think it was possible for man to destroy the fish in the sea. That point was very shortly and ably put in a lecture which Professor Huxley gave at Norwich. He said there were a number of enemies of the herring: the cod fish, birds, and everything else we have heard of, and if man took so many herrings out of the sea, it was a sort of co-operative society, those others herring fisheries getting so much less; but as for any idea of destroying deep sea fisheries, from the knowledge we possessed he was diametrically opposed to the opinion expressed by Dr. Day and some other gentlemen, and he believed that more investigation would only show that it was absolutely impossible. Still, he admitted it was a subject which ought to be discussed, and he was glad to hear their opinion upon it. He did not think it was possible to supply the markets now by simple inshore fishing, and while he admitted that to some extent those fisheries might be injured, much more harm was done to fisheries in general by trying to protect them, than any good which might be supposed to be effected by increasing the inshore fisheries. It was true that restrictive legislation had not been put in force in all cases, but both the chairman and himself had alluded to the very great mischief which was done on the west coast of Scotland, for the population of the western islands were reduced almost to starvation by laws which did absolutely no good to the fisheries. The Executive Committee would pay every attention to the suggestion made by Mr. Johnson with reference to bringing the matters he mentioned more fully before the public. In conclusion, he begged to propose a vote of thanks to the Chairman, who, he was glad to think, as a scientific authority, as well as a man of practical knowledge, entirely agreed with him on the controverted question which had been raised.

Mr. BRUCE, M.P., seconded the motion. Having the honour to represent in the House of Commons a number of fishermen located on the shores of the Firth of Forth, he had naturally listened with great interest to the discussion, and he might say that was one of those places where the herring fishing used to be prosecuted with greater success, but which appeared to some extent to have been deserted of late years by the herrings. The reasons for this were not very well known, but he was glad to say that the fishermen in that quarter had not given up fishing, but had improved their boats and gone farther out to sea to carry on their industry. Whatever else they might differ about, all would agree that it was of the greatest importance that a gentleman of such ability as Sir Lyon Playfair should give his mind to the study of these subjects, and that nothing but good could result from his investigations.

Mr. WILMOT asked leave to add, in explanation, that the salt-water herring fisheries were more extensive than the whole of those on the shores of Great Britain, and that whilst he spoke of the fresh-water lakes Mr. MacLelan had spoken of the herrings of the sea.

The vote of thanks having been carried unanimously,

The CHAIRMAN, in responding, assured Dr. Day that the last thing he desired was to stop discussion by speaking *ex cathedrâ*, but, as late Chairman of the House of Commons, he knew that having spoken then he could not speak again, and so was obliged to say all he had to say; but it was with the desire of eliciting discussion, and not putting an end to it. He had been delighted to hear the different opinions given by different speakers, and he was quite sure the public would profit very much by the different views put forward.

International Fisheries Exhibition,
LONDON, 1883.

SCOTCH EAST COAST,

ORKNEY AND SHETLAND, LEWIS AND BARRA

HERRING FISHING.

BY

W. S. MILN.

[*PRIZE ESSAY.*]

LONDON:
WILLIAM CLOWES AND SONS, LIMITED,
13 CHARING CROSS, S.W.
1884.

LONDON :
PRINTED BY WILLIAM CLOWES AND SONS, LIMITED,
STAMFORD STREET AND CHARING CROSS.

THE SCOTCH EAST COAST HERRING FISHING.

Fishermen — Numbers Employed — Habits and Social Condition—Qualities and Characteristics—Wealth.

The number of fishermen actively employed in the herring fishings during the seasons, from Northumberland to, and including, Wick, and at Orkney and Shetland, and Lewis and Barra in the Hebrides, can be safely estimated at over 45,000 men and boys.

The habits of fishermen are distinctly discernible as pertaining to a broad sectarianism. Individually, their idea of bodily comfort consists in having on a superabundance of clothes. Even during the warm months of July and August, whilst working hard in hoisting their catch to the carts on the quay, it is ridiculous the amount of clothing they have on them. The great beads of sweat pouring down their faces and bodies, and the ofttimes visible steaming therefrom, does not convince them that they are overclad. 'Tis a pity they do not regulate their dress in accordance with the weather, as it is obvious that over-burdening one's self with clothing is unhealthy, and weakening to the body, especially during warm weather. What a contrast to the French fishermen;—they having a tendency to underclothe themselves, judging by their open-breasted semmit, or shirt. Our fishermen are likewise very much needing a thorough lecturing and training in the art of making clean by a judicious and plentiful use of soap and water, and an occasional total immersion. The fisherwomen might follow the example also with advantage. Of course there are exceptions, and they deserve commendation for their cleanliness. Their homes are comfortable, but are slightly overcrowded, generally clean, and the furniture more ancient than modern. Fish is their great sustenance, but when they are at the fishing centres the beef they then use makes up for the scarcity whilst at home during the winter. It is necessary to give a justly merited warning and particularly required denunciation regarding overcrowding at the large centres, such as Fraserburgh, Peterhead, Wick, during the season. House proprietors and lodging-house keepers are more to blame than the fishermen, as they should be made to provide suitable accommodation if they are to be allowed to lodge fishermen and their families. As for the fishermen, poor simple people, they are only too glad to secure any shelter during their temporary residence, no matter how filthy. The accommodation being limited, overcrowding is general, and the manner of their huddling together in outhouses, stores, lofts, and even worse places, is a disgrace to civilisation. To know about, and to have seen the overcrowding and filth, and to have inhaled the nauseous vapours when passing these temporary abodes, gives one the feeling that such living is not only disgusting, but degrading. Such mode of living is not the fishermen's choice, but is forced on them as a necessity. It is high time that a Parliamentary Commission be appointed to examine and report upon the accommodation available for the fisher people at the various herring fishing stations. Let their visit take place during the heat of a season, and the disclosures will show an indecency and moral degradation of a most appalling nature. One visit would certainly be sufficient, and would be the means of raising the fishing community from a backward and unwholesome living, to one more healthy and modern.

The qualities and characteristics of fishermen may also be said to be sectarian. Amongst the Highlanders intemperance is the prevailing vice, but it is gratifying to observe the wonderful alteration that is gradually making itself visible in their sect, and which augurs well for the hope that in the near future our fishermen will be known as a temperate race of men. Religion has also a considerable part of their attention. They are chiefly connected with the Gaelic Church. The southern fishermen are pretty well mixed up with all the denominations. Missionary work receives good support, is beneficial, and has a splendid ground to work upon. However, the fishermen, notwithstanding their regular church attendance and adhesiveness to their creeds—seeming equal to fanaticism—are found, on a close observation of their daily life, to be divided thus, one-third zealous, God-fearing, and good living men, while the other two-thirds are not, and a great part are (I am sorry to have to say it) in disposition inclined to the opposite direction. I draw my conclusions from close observance. Obstinacy in argument is a prominent characteristic. There is also a deep vindictiveness and revengefulness in their natures against those whom they may deem enemies. Without flattery, let us glance at the good qualities of our fishermen. To their employers they are respectful, and self-knowing, subservient; hard working and energetic in their occupation;

cautious (after a manner, ofttimes unnecessarily and unfittingly so); bold and daring in presence of danger; affectionate to their wives and children; ambitious to be affluent, and desirous to keep on a level with the times; but withal, retaining a strict adhesion to their caste.

Wealth is pretty equally divided. Well-to-do fishermen are sure to possess, first, a house and furniture; second, boat and gear, or perhaps shares of a large and a small boat; third, nets, lines, and other fishing materials. The heads of families are generally tolerably comfortable as regards means. A small proportion may, through unfortunate circumstances, be poor for a time, but perseverance soon overcomes the poverty. The various banks receive a goodly amount of money on deposit from them; and when we consider that mostly all the houses in the fishing villages which they inhabit belong to themselves for the greater part, we must allow that as a class they are both powerful and rich. Young fishermen, as they earn and save money, invest it in their fathers' or relatives' boats, thereby securing an interest in the boat, and therefore in the industry. They earn and save more money than any other class in Scotland, and as fortune and hard work seem to go hand in hand, the energy and instinctive ambition for supremacy entitles us to reasonably expect a continuous and progressive prosperity in the future.

FISHING MATERIAL—BOATS AND GEAR—NETS—BASKETS AND SPADES—METHOD OF CATCH—DELIVERY.

Fifteen years ago the fishing boats were principally those which we know now under the name of the "skaffie," a fast sailing, but unhandy and very much inferior boat compared with the present new style. The cost of a

XI.-23. Plate I.

"skaffie" boat would then range from £175 to £210. The "KY"—i.e. Kirkcaldy style, is the most popular at present. They are first-class built, and will carry with comfort a catch of 70 to 100 crans of herrings, equal to 8 to 15 tons. Their dimensions and "rig" make them suitable for a further from shore fishing than the "skaffie." According to the newest improvements and additional appliances, a first-class "KY" style of boat would cost over £300. There have been a good many highly superior boats launched during the past two or three years, their shape slightly differing from the "KY" style, but they are materially of the same class, with the exception that they are better deck-built and have the most modern appliances. They cost £20 to £50 more than the average "KY." Gear comprises sails, ropes, anchors, chains, oars, &c., and their cost is included in the price of the boat. The following table shows the exact number of boats fishing at each station, from Northumberland to Shetland, and including Lewis and Barra, for the past five years.

Stations and Districts.	1878.	1879.	1880.	1881.	1882.
WICK to Keiss	579	597	655	570	600
Lybster and Clyth	131	132	141	147	140
Forse Station	14	10	9	4	4
Latheronwheel Station	16	15	15	15	13
Dunbeath Station	39	40	32	34	31
Helmsdale Station	160	130	170	145	160
Portmahomack Station	26	16	22	28	30
Burghead and Hopeman Station	34	17	47	45	50
Lossiemouth Station	13	24	42	47	42
Buckie District	32	26	75	67	95
Portsoy Station	35	38	39	40	46
Whitehills Station	9	13	10	10	12

Stations and Districts.	1878.	1879.	1880.	1881.	1882.
Banff Station	2	9	8	11	15
Macduff Station	36	52	41	39	66
Gardenstown Station	25	49	36	53	41
Fraserburgh District	879	1006	944	1007	900
Peterhead District	683	768	716	849	822
Aberdeen District	490	400	361	501	482
Stonehaven District	..	..	..	..	101
Montrose District	233	204	244	225	166
Anstruther District.	35	36	70	36	20
Leith to Dunbar	40	65	60	60	45
Eyemouth District	321	233	373	282	381
Orkney Islands	192	183	170	180	197
Shetland Islands	120	206	206	284	372
Lewis and Barra	871	1084	1381	1285	1300

Taking the year 1882, we have 6131 boats, which, calculated at an average cost of £275 per boat including gear, gives the handsome capital of £1,686,025 sterling invested solely by fishermen in these herring boats, altogether exclusive of nets. It is pleasing to relate that these boats are being covered against loss by Insurance.

There is now no regulation size of mesh or net. The net as bought from the manufacturer is 60 yards in length, but when hung on the back rope is only equal to 40 yards long. The depth is on average about 12 yards. The cotton threads comprising the net are of 9, 12, 15, 18, and 21 ply. The mesh is about 1 square inch, measured from knot to knot, and commonly there are 32, 33, and 34 meshes in the yard. As the nets get older, through shrinking, there are 34 to 38, and even 40 meshes to the yard. During a fair fishing the new nets are regularly "barked" once a fortnight. Old nets require "barking" only once a month. "Barking" is the process of browning the nets by boiling them in cutch. The "swing rope" is a rope attached to the nets from the boat and is their safeguard, so to speak. The price of a net is in the meantime 33*s.*, which, together with mounting 4*s.* 6*d.* + head rope 12*s.* 6*d.* + buoy 4*s.* 6*d.* + floats 3*s.* + bark 3*s.* 9*d.* + fishermen's labour estimated at 8*s.* 9*d.* = £3 10*s.*; and therefore that is the sum to be paid for a fair average quality net ready for use. A boat carries from 25 to 50 nets, and that quantity is termed a "fleet." Making the lowest possible estimates appear by allowing only 25 nets to each boat, we have in use 153,275 nets, which at £3 10*s.* per net, gives the value of £536,462 sterling.

The baskets for the measuring of the herrings are supplied by the curer, and, sad to relate, in too many cases are slightly larger than the regulation size. The remedy lies with the fishermen, and they have themselves to blame if they do not take advantage thereof. The regulation measurement of the cran is $37\frac{1}{2}$ gallons imperial standard measurement. There are 4 baskets to the cran, and each basket is exactly one-fourth of the aforementioned required standard measurement. In shape they resemble a common tub, but are wicker-worked, having in circumference two or three inches more at top than bottom. The rim of the basket is heavy worked and has two handles for fixing the hoisting rope and lifting. There requires to be on board the boat from two to four spades or scoops for shovelling the herrings into the baskets. Formerly they were entirely wooden, but now the heads are of zinc. The fishermen supply these spades; they cost from 2*s.* 6*d.* to 3*s.* each. Baskets cost about 2*s.* each. Making a fair allowance for each boat we find that these articles presently in use would give a money value of £5000.

Method of catch is thus explained: the boat and crew being ready to proceed to sea the crew get aboard and commence to "red," i.e. fold the nets in methodical succession, head-rope being to "stern," and foot-rope to "bow." To counteract the weight and position of the nets stones are used to balance. That finished, the boat is pushed or rowed out of the harbour, sail is hoisted, and, according to the state of wind and tide, is steered out to the fishing grounds. Arrived there, sail is lowered, and the nets "cast" or "shot" over the starboard side of the boat. The "watch" is set. Shortly before sunrise, and with the disappearance of the phosphoric light, the nets are hauled aboard and the herrings are shaken, weather permitting, from the nets into the "hold," and the nets folded methodically. Should the sea be rough when the hauling takes place, the nets cannot be shaken; but that no time may be lost, and to admit of the herrings being delivered in best possible condition, the fishermen always endeavour to have their nets shaken as they approach the harbour.

Delivery is here to be understood as from the boat to the carts on the quay. The fishermen shovel the herrings into the baskets and hoist them by means of ropes running through a "pulley" attached to the top of the boat's mast. When on a level with the quay, the carter, who has a rope fixed to the basket rope, draws to him, and the contents are emptied into his cart. A crew consists of five or six men and a boy, and in delivering the herrings, half of them attend to the filling of the baskets, and the other half to the hoisting. All have hard work, and there is no stoppage till every herring is delivered. The hoisting tells severely on the hands, and is not improved by the curious use of heavy worsted "mits" or gloves so often seen worn by the "hoisters."

FISH-CURERS—CURING YARDS—PLANT—COOPERS—ORAMEN—GUTTERS—KIPPERERS AND SMOKERS—CARTAGE—STOCK.

There are about 500 firms engaged in the herring curing trade on the East Coast, Orkney and Shetland, Lewis and Barra. The capital invested would amount to from £720,000 to £1,000,000 sterling. Of all classes they are always the most dependent, entirely relying on the sea's product; independent, meantime, by their position and standing; enterprising yet rash and speculative—none more so. They are industrious, and are deserving of the country's best thanks for so carefully, laboriously, even expensively, but not withal judiciously, conducting their business, the methods and results of which are so highly gratifying as to command the esteem of millions of people at home and abroad. They have raised to a high pinnacle the fame of the Scotch herring trade, and long may they preserve the position and honour.

Presuming that a herring curer has fully made up his mind as to the extent of his business, let us glance at his requirements. In the first place it is necessary that a suitable "stance" be procured, near or at the harbour, whereon the yard is to be erected. Supplies of wood (staves) and hoops are ordered, and suitable 'plant' is bought. The coopers are engaged. Boat-engaging time comes on, and the curer looks out for the good boats, and endeavours to engage them. After fixing his boats, he gives his orders for the salt required. If he is a practical curer and cooper he assists in the cutting and making of heads for the barrels, and otherwise superintends the business.

Curing yards are commonly square shaped. The buildings constituting a yard differ very much, in fact every locality has a different style. At Fraserburgh and Peterhead some very fine yards have been built lately. The frontages are of stone, and perhaps several stores are also of stone, but generally there are one or more wooden erections, stones, kilns, or coverings. At Pointlaw, Aberdeen, there are thirty-five yards, which are all, without exception, built of wood. This is owing to the short leases obtainable from the Harbour Commissioners. Pointlaw is part of the reclaimed ground at the Inches, and it is specially set apart for fish-curing.

The portion fronting the street or lane is generally the "gutting shed." Through a swing door or doors in the front of this shed the herrings are tumbled promiscuously, and fall into a large square box, or tank, called a "farlin," i.e. a repository for the herrings, where they are "roused," and await the process of gutting. Adjoining is the "cooperage." In front thereof, at a distance of a few yards, is the "firing-plate and truss-hoops." Sufficient storage accommodation is required for the barrels, salt, hoops and staves. Of late I have noticed an improvement in the gutting-sheds; I refer to the laying of the floors with concrete. It is worthy of mention that the fish-curers at Shetland, while laying out capital on their yards, are likewise under the necessity of providing "jetties," or landing slips near their stations at their own expense. I sincerely trust their enterprise will be rewarded. Shetland may be said to have risen within the past two years from insignificance to eminence. Whereas last year curing was carried on under difficulty, the catch being rather too heavy to be worked properly, the temporary curing yards seeming swamps, shipment difficult, communication limited, and

XI.-23.
Plate II.

house accommodation more so, this year the curers will have nearly all the advantages to be had at home. The telegraph service is extended, as also steamer and land communication. Several substantial "jetties" have been built, and likewise good curing yards have been put up. Even the remote parts of the islands have every prospect of seeing a general merchant open business when the fishing begins. Barra, on the west coast, is by Lady Gordon Cathcart's assistance gradually rising from obscurity to significance, and although last year was a failure, it is to be hoped that the future fishings will prove a steady increase compared to the former years. Stornoway has now assumed the supremacy of the west coast, and has a large trade. On account of the Barra failure last season, Stornoway being extra-well fished, it is likely that there will be a great increase of boats next season (1883). The west coast fishing is for the greater part prosecuted by east coast curers, and, with the exception of Stornoway, all the yards are of a temporary character.

Plant consists of farlins (already described); small tubs or baskets for the various selections; large rousing tub; hoop-bending mill, costs about £11 to £15; head-boring mill, costs about £4 or £5; grindstone for sharpening tools; firing-plate and truss-hoops; crisset and fender; steep for soaking hoops; head and side jointers; head and side planes, or pluckers; adze for notching hoops; trussing hammer and drivers; shore, croze, and flencher or chime-howl; crumb or champhering-knife, head-knife, draw-knife; compass for taking the circumference of the barrel-heads; head and crosscut saws; two bits for boring the bung and spile holes; and stave-moulding axe, saw stool, head-cleaning board, dowl-dropper, and diagonal rod. Where there are kilns there are also required steeps for pickling the herrings, tenters or spits for hanging the herrings while being smoked, together with other small utensils which are hardly worth mentioning. Be it understood that quantities of the above articles are required according to the extent of the business.

The coopers steadily employed in the trade are about 3000 in number, including apprentices. During the herring fishing the journeymen, on an average, receive 33*s.* to 35*s.* per week. Foremen a few shillings more. During the winter their wages are earned on the work done. The principal employment then is barrel-making. A good man can make by steady work 24 barrels a week. The price for making a barrel is 1*s.*, and therefore the cooper can earn 24*s.* per week by steady work. He has a very responsible position, and is in reality the practical fish-curer. First, there is the necessity of making his barrels the exact regulation size, and showing an apparent good workmanship, tight fitting and well hooped. Second, care and punctiliousness in "rousing," i.e. salting to keep the herrings in good condition, till convenient to be gutted, and during the process of gutting. Third, the keeping in good working order all plant, and especially the farlins, tubs and gutting knives, and the superintending of gutting, selection, laying, and packing. Fourth, he has to devote particular attention to the pickling and filling up, and presentation for the brand. Although not receiving a remuneration equal in comparison to the amount of labour and responsibility, still, greatly to their credit, they are a contented, hardworking, thrifty, and energetic class of men, and by their excellent service are the instruments in making for the Scotch cure such a high fame as it has.

Oramen are only employed during the herring fishing season ; 400 or 500 might be the estimate of the numbers employed. Their wages are about 20s. per week, and they are engaged to assist the coopers, and make themselves generally useful in the yard. Many of them are engaged as "cranners," that is, to attend to the delivery of the herrings from the boats, keep correct count of the baskets emptied into the carts, and in particular to see that the baskets are properly filled, and otherwise look to the interests of the fish-curer he is in service with. They are mostly of the labouring class, or persons out of employment.

"Gutters" are those engaged to gut the herrings on their arrival at the curing-yard. Women are employed as gutters. The fish-curer engages a "crew" of women for each boat. A crew consists of three persons. Two gut, and the other one packs the herrings gutted by them. There are over 20,000 women employed during the season. Their wages are at the rate of 8d. per barrel, gutting and packing, per crew. Those who are fortunately with a curer having a large average make a good sum of money for the season, but there are also those unfortunately with a curer with a poor average, and therefore their wages are comparatively small. The gutting of herrings is a laborious occupation. It is common in a yard to hear women singing cheerily at their work, they having commenced at mid-day and continued work in the same bent-figured attitude till the early hours next morning. Once commenced, there is *no* stoppage till the finish. While the herrings are before them, money is to be made. Work is no object. When the curer engages the gutting women, they are paid "arle" money of from 35s. to 55s. each woman, according to their known qualifications as "gutters."

Kipperers and smokers have quite a different class of work from the gutters. Kipperers, in the first place, have to "split" the herrings, and afterwards have to pack them into the boxes. They are generally engaged for about 17s. per week, but sometimes we find them working for 3d. per hour.

Smokers are the men employed to attend to the smoking, hanging up, and taking down of the herrings. They get about 27s. to 36s. per week, and considering the heavy work they are not overpaid. They are continually "heaping" the fires, and one can easily imagine the unwholesome vapours and heat to be simply stifling. It only requires an "anxious inquirer" to put his head in at the door of a smoke-house to convince him that a smoker's duties are onerous, most trying to the health, and exceedingly dangerous.

For cartage of the herrings from the boats to the yard, and when cured from the yard to ship's side for export, contracts are entered into between the curer and carter. The contract rates vary at all centres, but 2d. per cran from the boat to the yard, and 3d. per barrel from the yard to ship's side, may be given as the likeliest average. The best style of bulk herring cart is a long, even-balanced body-cart, and is specially adapted for the trade. A temporary division in the middle of a common cart prevents the herrings from slipping backwards, thereby tending to overbalance the cart and spill the herrings. For conveying barrels a "lorry" is the best. The income derived from the cartage of herrings for the past few years is not less than £15,000 per annum.

The principal articles of a herring curer's stock are staves and heading, hoops and salt. The curer may procure billet-wood and cut into staves by his own order; but generally the staves are delivered at the yard ready to be worked. The various woods used for barrel-making in the order of their value are larch, birch, ash, spruce, and Scotch fir. Larch is the dearest wood, and undoubtedly makes the finest barrels; costs from 80s. to 90s. per 1000 feet, and on account of its dearness is not so much used as it deserves to be. Birch is the medium quality, and is the most popular. Perhaps half of all the barrels made are of birch. Our greatest supplies are from Norway; Mandal and Pörsgrund shipping the best qualities. Our home supplies are indeed very small, and there is nothing in the quality of the home birch that particularly calls for comment. The price is at present firm at 75s. per 1000 feet. Spruce and common fir have of late years come much into use, and are appreciated on account of cheapness. Likewise the curers can be supplied by the neighbouring wood merchants at such times as they may require, and in small quantities. The price is from 60s. to 65s. per 1000 feet. These woods are very soft compared to larch or birch; and after the barrel has been filled with herrings and lain for 2 or 3 months in store, it is found that the pickle has become absorbed in the wood, the barrel has expanded, and therefore the herrings present a slackened appearance. I give it as my opinion that the less fir barrels are used the better for the trade. The curers may save a little in the price of the *barrel*, but they will certainly lose more than the amount in the sale of the barrels of herrings, for the simple reason that the German herring dealers have a dislike to fir barrels. It takes about 16 to 20 staves to make one barrel. 1000 feet of staves and 250 feet of heading will give about 70 barrels on an average. The nett cost of a barrel is from 3s. 3d. to 3s. 6d. according to the quality of the wood used. By these figures I estimate that it costs over £125,000 every year to prepare the stock of barrels for this herring fishing.

The hoops required for the barrel are in length $7\frac{1}{4}$ feet, are about $\frac{1}{4}$ inch thick, and vary in breadth from $\frac{3}{4}$ to 1 inch.

They are of wood, and are principally either of ash, birch, elm, willow, and hazel. The great supply of hoops are bought through London merchants, and are collected by them from all parts. The finest finished hoops come from Surrey. The cash price of hoops is for whole barrel 34*s.*, and for half-barrel 25*s.* f.o.b. London. From 16 to 18 hoops are required for each barrel. The money value for the total used during each year is not under £45,000.

The salt required by the curer is generally ordered about or immediately after the new year, and for delivery a week or two before the early fishing commences. The supply is calculated at from 12 to 15 tons of salt to the boat for a fair average fishing. Salt is in a great measure the responsible element in the cure, and it is therefore in the best interests of the curer to procure the best salt suitable for curing purposes. For " rousing," common salt is quite good enough, but for " packing and filling up " a great grained salt is required—first quality—is the proper requisite. Lisbon and St. Ubes salt has found much favour as a splendid salt for " packing," and on the west coast is much appreciated. However, this salt is not so much dealt in as its quality would warrant, but that is probably on account of the risk, measurement instead of weight, or a disinclination, from lack of sufficient profit, to deal therewith by the seller on this side. German salt has been tried at one or two stations, and its qualities proven satisfactory. It is, however, still in its infancy, and from all appearance may take some little time to get out of it on account of prejudice. I have had the pleasure of myself introducing it at Aberdeen, having contracted for 150 tons, for July delivery. This salt is exclusively for packing and filling up. It is beautifully clear, great grained, and stands an excellent analysis.

Fishermen's Herring Shovel.
Do.   Do.   Basket.
Gutting-Women's Salt-Scoop.
Do.   Knife.
East Coast Regulation-sized Herring Barrel
and Head, shewing formation.

Engagements between Curer and Fisher—Bounty System—Arles and Dates of Agreement.

The bounty system has been in force for a great length of time. From 1720 (perhaps before that time) to 1830 there were bounties at irregular periods given by Government to aid in the further development and extension of the trade. For interesting examples, I quote the following. In the year 1727 a Board of Trustees was appointed to manage the sum of £20,000 per annum allowed by the Government from Scotch Revenue (*vide* Act, 23 Geo. II.). Great encouragements were given and assistance rendered in floating the "Free British White Herring Company," whose capital was £500,000. Bounty was then paid at 30s. per ton on "busses" from 20 to 80 tons burthen. The year 1757 saw the bounty at 50s. per ton. We read of the Scotch having earned bounty in 1767, amounting to £31,396, but in 1781 only £9,674. In 1782 the bounty was reduced to 30s., not on the tonnage now, but on the ton of fish delivered. In 1808 we know of it having been paid in the form of 2s. for every barrel qualified, presented, and receiving the Government brand. It was raised to 4s. in 1815, and altogether withdrawn in 1830. Such was the bounty system of the olden times. Good in its way, and having its origin in the best of intentions—viz. to promote the development, and by its monetary assistance to encourage the trade.

The modern system is quite different, and to my seeming is a dangerous practice. It is a "bond," or "service," money paid by the herring curer to the fishers owning the boat as the part price of the contract. The following table shows the average amount of bounty per boat paid during the past six years. Before then the bounties were comparatively small, even as low as £5.

	1877.	1878.	1879.	1880.	1881.	1882.
Bounty paid	£20	£30	£40	£20	£40	£48

The fluctuations in bounty payments are entirely caused by the preceding year's catch and prices. Therefore the payments are purely speculative as to probable rise or fall for the coming year. A glance at the prices here given from the principal market—Stettin—will tend to prove this.

The quotations on 31st December were as follows:—

(Calculate 20½ mks. to £1.)

In	1877.	1878.	1879.	1880.	1881.	1882.
	M.	M.	M.	M.	M.	M.
Scotch Crownfulls	44	38	52½–53	29–30	40½–41	38½–39
,, Crown Matties	29	27–28	34–37	21–23	34–35	31–32
,, ,, Mixed	27	25–26	35–37	22½–23½	32½–34	31
,, ,, Spents	26	25–26	37½–38	22½	31½	31

The curers argue that to procure good boats good bounties must be paid. If bounties of a necessity must be given, then I agree with them. But why should bounties be paid? For example, take two boats both getting the same amount of bounty. One takes 100 crans, and the other 200 crans; in which case it would appear reasonable to expect that the catch of 100 crans should only receive half the bounty of the other; but it is not so. They both have the same bounty, but the one boat's fish is considerably dearer than the other; this to show that the bounty is not well or even-balanced. Again, if a curer has engaged eleven boats this year, he has paid out of his capital slightly more than £500 six or seven months before the fishing commences. There is an obvious risk in this speculative payment, and there is a chance of its being entirely lost. For instance, the Barra fishing last year (1882) was a complete failure. The bounty was £40 per boat. The curer's loss was averaged at £55 per boat. Had no bounty been paid, the loss would have only been £15 per boat.

To the fishermen this payment of bounty is supposed to assist them in passing through the winter, and to allow of improvements to their boats. As presents to the fishermen, without conditions attached thereto, such payments would be too highly commendable. But why not make this payment, if necessarily required by the fishermen, simply an advance to be repaid out of earnings? In some instances the bounty is misapplied, and it has been known to encourage laziness amongst the crews, especially in the early weeks of the fishing, when the cran is cheaper than in the regular set time. Bounties will come to a sudden stop the first year there is a backward and losing fishing. At present a good year to the curer means a greater speculative payment for the one that is to come, and that without any augury as to an equivalent return.

Arles are usually paid by the curer to the fisher over and above the bounty when the engagements are entered into. The arles are this year £1 per boat. As the fisher owning the boat has to "arle" his crew, I presume the £1 is given for that purpose.

The average bounty, including arles, paid on the east coast for the coming season, 1883, is about £48 per boat; inferior boats having £35 to £45; good boats £45 to £50; and first-class boats £50 to £53. Many boats are this year to commence fishing on the 1st July, but the engaged early fishing is from the 8th or 10th July till the 16th or 18th

July. The prices at these dates are 11s. to 14s. per cran. The regular fishing commences on the 16th to 18th July, and continues thereafter for eight weeks, or till the complement of 200 crans is delivered. In the event of a boat making its complement before the eight weeks are over, and exceeds it, the herrings can be taken by the curer at a less rate— 14s. or 15s. per cran, but the curer is not bound to take them. The early fishing at Shetland commences this year during the first week of June. The price is 14s. or 15s. for the first 100 crans. The curers have it in their option to take more herrings at that money, or not. The regular fishing commences on the 1st July, and the price is 20s. for the first 250 crans. It is again in the curer's option to take more or not. The bounty and arles is on average £32 per boat. The native Shetland boats receive no bounty, and are engaged on the same terms as the "strangers." Curers on the mainland must have two stations (one on the west side, Scalloway, and one on the east side, Lerwick). This is accounted for by the theory that the herrings are only to be found on the west side during the first half of the season, and on the east side during the latter half. This theory may be correct or not, but at all events the curers and fishermen believe in it, and therefore the boats fish at two places, but under one agreement. The extension of the herring fishery at the North Isles only dates from last year. There are few stations on the west side, but all the season herrings were plentiful on the east side both early and late. The west coast fishing commences in the beginning of May, but the engagements generally run from the 10th May, the price being 15s. per cran. The regular fishing is from the 20th May till the end of June, and the price is 20s. per cran. The average bounty at Stornoway is £35 per boat, and at Barra £45 per boat. According to qualifications the prices are low or high. The inferior boats have as low as £30, and first-class boats as high as £50.

Copy of Agreement general with Fish-curers and Fishermen.

"Sir,

"We, the undersigned crew of herring fishermen, having good boats and proper fleets of nets in our possession, hereby agree diligently and faithfully to prosecute the herring fishing for you at ——— and deliver to you all herrings we catch as per agreement during herring fishing season 188 commencing on the ——— July at ——— shillings per cran, till ——— July, and from that date until eight weeks, at the rate of ——— shillings per cran for two hundred crans, and ——— shillings for all crans afterwards. All the herrings to be delivered in good (fisherman's) workmanship order and condition, before ——— P.M. of the day after which we leave the harbour for the fishing grounds.

"Besides the above rates per cran we receive ——— as bounty and earnest. You supply net ground and cartage of fish and nets. All herrings not up to terms of agreement we will offer you at what they are worth."

> 6d.
> Agreement Stamp.

CURING — FRESHING — KIPPERING — RED HERRINGS— TINNING—FAMOUS PICKLE CURE—A FEW REMARKS AS TO THE UTILITY OF FISH OFFAL.

The trade in sending to the English markets, inland towns, and the larger country villages, receives a good deal of attention, and is very lucrative, unless there be a heavy fishing, and therefore a probable glut. There are only a few fish-curers who work this "fresh trade." It is principally carried on by fresh-fish buyers, and they buy from the boats or the curers their daily supplies at prices according to the markets and prospects. Stornoway in particular does a large "freshing" business. To explain the "freshing," let us suppose a supply of herrings has been got. They are "roused" and well laid with small grained salt; straw, and perhaps matting, is put over the top of the barrel mouth and made firm. Boxes, barrels, or tubs will do, although iron-hooped boxes are the correct thing—and all that is wanted is expeditious transmission to the consignee.

There are a good many curers engaged in making kippers. A few of the many are long established, and therefore have a fairly wide known popularity as to their cure and merits. This coming season will see a great extension in kippering, as at large stations, such as Montrose, Aberdeen, Peterhead, Fraserburgh, Lerwick, and Stornoway, there are more curers entering on this branch of the trade. "Kippers" are at present a very popular edible, but there is only a limited home consumption, and as they do not keep their condition after two or three weeks, there is a danger in too fast extension, which will without doubt bring down the prices, and probably overstock the markets. It must be remembered also that the English cure a large portion of their catch in this style, and will prove dangerous competitors.

Red herrings are not cured so much for the home markets as for foreign. The countries around the Mediterranean are the largest consumers, and prices therefrom are good. The cure is thus described. The herrings are soaked in salt and saltpetre till they are rigid. The pickle is then removed. They are hung on the spits for a few days, and afterwards smoked until they are of the required colour. It takes eight or nine days to cure red herrings properly.

The tinning of herrings for the greater part is confined to Aberdeen, and Australia is the great market. Last year (1882) there were close on $2\frac{1}{4}$ millions of tins exported from Aberdeen for the various warm countries. There are from three to five herrings in a tin, and the tin and herrings weigh 1 lb. The process of curing and putting up is pretty much kept secret, and in case of mistakes I had better not endeavour to describe the method.

The famous Scotch pickle cure, the most important of all methods, now deserves special reference. The "pickle cure" was first practised as an article of trade in Holland in the year 1307. Immediately on the herrings being delivered by the carter at the yard, and deposited or "tumbled" into the farlin, i.e. gutting-tub, the coopers are careful to sprinkle them well with salt. This sprinkling of salt—called "rousing"—preserves and revives the condition of the herrings while they are being gutted. The gutting women lose no time in commencing their work. With their short knife in the right hand, and the herring in their left, they, by a dexterous and experienced movement withdraw the viscera and gills. All bloody matter is included therewith, and its withdrawal prevents the fish from turning a sickly colour, they would otherwise turn if the bloody matter remained. First-class cured fish keep beautifully clear and free from smell for nine or twelve months. After that time an unhealthy appearance makes itself manifest. As the herrings are gutted they are dropped into tubs according to their qualities. These tubs are placed close to the large gutting-box or farlin, and there is one for every selection. The gutters should be most particular in selection. The small tubs are carried by the "packers" to where the packing is taking place—generally in the centre, or open part of the yard—and emptied into a larger tub. Here they are again "roused." Two or three turns over with the hands is sufficient. In packing, the herrings are "laid" on their backs, and the packer sees that a proper quantity of salt is sprinkled over every tier. Attention is paid to pressing and refilling after the barrel has stood for a few days. Whereas small grained salt is the best for rousing, great grained salt is necessary for laying and packing. The various selections of the pickle cure on the east coast and Shetland are—1st, Fulls, i.e. full-sized, having roe or milt developed; 2nd, Matties, i.e. undersized, roe and milt immature; 3rd, Spent, i.e. spawned fish; 4th, Tornbellies, i.e. fish either split in the side, breast, or belly, while being gutted or torn in these parts in being shaken from the nets. The curers at various intervals—commonly near the end of the season—have another selection, viz. Mixed, i.e. matties and spents in equal quantities to be packed promiscuously in the same barrel. This mixed cure finds much favour with the North German and Russian dealers. I may also mention that since 1880—the disputing year—many curers are making two selections of the "fulls," viz. large fulls and medium fulls. This is praiseworthy of the curers, and in my opinion is the only way to keep the Mattie selection entirely distinct. Formerly, in a barrel of matties there was an equal—or very nearly so—quantity of small fulls. Such should not be. I say that immature fish—" matties "—should be kept separate from mature fish, even though the mature fish be small sized.

As the fish offal accumulates, it is carefully collected and transferred to old barrels set apart for that purpose. A barrel of herring offal realises from 1s. to 1s. 6d. per barrel. In the beginning of the season the farmers contract for a certain supply. Fish offal as a manure is now well known and appreciated as a good crop-raising stimulant. It is estimated that at the lowest possible over 75,000 barrels were taken delivery of by farmers on the east coast of Scotland alone, and the money value thereof to be not less than £5000 sterling. In its raw state the offal is, in the event of its too heavy application to the soil, apt to "burn." To prevent this burning it is apparent that it must have a compost. Our fishing centres should not be without manufactories for the drying and compressing of offal with such composts as, say, peat-moss, road sweepings, fine ashes and cinders from gasworks, or even from the common ash-pits. The composts are easily obtained, would make a capital all round manure, and for cheapness hardly to be beaten.

The Branding System—History—The Brand Explained—Statistics—Qualifications.

In the 36th clause of Act of Parliament, 1808, we first hear of a brand on herrings. The presentment of a barrel of herrings of sufficient merit to receive the branding stamp thereon entitled the curer to the sum of 2s. In

1815, that sum was raised to 4s., and thereat remained till 1830, at which date it was altogether withdrawn, but branding under the old regulations still continued. In 1859, a Parliamentary Commission of Enquiry reported favourably on the brand, and gave it as their opinion that the system of branding was beneficial in the interests of the curers, was a great facilitator of business—more especially in the foreign export trade—and was likewise a guarantee for the contents of the barrel and also the quality of the fish therein. A fee of 4d. per barrel branded was then imposed, and remains in force at this present day. Only lately has the brand received another vote of confidence, as it were. I refer to the report of the Select Committee appointed by the House of Commons in March 1881, to enquire into the expediency of continuing the system of branding herrings, &c. Their voting was as 12 against 3 that the brand was deserving of continuance.

The brand is a guarantee that the barrel is of the legal standard measurement, and that the herrings, for quality, selection, and packing, are up to the requirements of the Scotch Fishery Board. The brand is given to only four selections, viz. fulls, matties, spents, and mixed. There are twenty-six districts, and the branding officers employed throughout the whole, in 1882, numbered thirty-seven. As branding is now extended to Shetland, whose rapid growth is so visibly apparent, an increase in the branding staff must necessarily take place. The herrings to be entitled to receive the brand must be properly cured and packed, and have lain in the barrel twelve* clear days from date of catch. The curer signs a request note to the officer stating the number of

---

* The Fishery Board stipulate that to receive the brand the herrings must have lain *ten* clear days, *exclusive of catch and packing*. I therefore feel justified in quoting *twelve* clear days from catch.

barrels he desires branded. This has the officer's due attention. Previous to the examination of the "parcel," the officer receives a declaration to the effect that the herrings have been cured conformably to the regulations set forth, and also gets payment of the branding fees. He proceeds to examine the parcel, and to those entitled applies the branding stamp. The curer has had a fire prepared wherein to heat the officer's branding-iron, and when the iron is red-hot it is applied to the barrel, leaving an impression similar to the one here given. Every selection has a different stamp.

The above is for Packed Matties, branded in 18–71, and the J J is the branding officer's initials. There is no brand given to the west coast herrings, nor is one required, as the herrings are not selected further than the curers deem expedient. Perhaps one-third may be selected, entitling them to the name of "prime" or "choice," the other two-thirds are packed promiscuously.

That the brand is highly appreciated, and yearly gaining in appreciation, the following results will sufficiently prove.

| | | | On Barrels. | | On Fees. | |
Year.	Barrels Branded.	Fees therefrom.	Increase.	Decrease.	Increase.	Decrease.
		£ s. d.			£ s. d.	£ s. d.
1859	158,676	2,644 12 0	...	...	...	...
1869	244,522½	4,075 7 6	85,846½	...	1,430 15 6	...
1879	342,323	5,705 7 8	97,800½	...	1,630 0 2	...
*1880	689,286	11,488 2 0	346,963	...	5,782 14 4	...
1881	494,182½	8,236 7 6	...	195,103½	...	3,251 14 6
1882	462,612½	7,710 4 2	...	31,570	...	526 3 4

* The fishing of 1880 was the heaviest on record, in fact it proved by its unexpectedness quite too much of a good thing. We must therefore not consider 1881 as a year of decline, but, as it were, calculate proportionately as an increase over 1879. While 1882 proves another decrease, it must be mentioned that the branding officers were most stringently exacting in fulfilment of their duties, and the rejections were more numerous than in former years. The tenor of the quality under the brand is, in my opinion, raised thereby, and a continued strictness under the regulations as to quality and selection makes us hopeful that the brand will score a further success, and still remain prosperous in itself. The Lybster to Helmsdale coast fishing proving a comparative failure also helps to account for the slight decrease.

The brand is an excellent trade-mark, and as such facilitates the buying and selling. This last year (1882) the buying and shipping of herrings was commenced and almost finished within a period of five months. The number of barrels exported is given as $782,290\frac{1}{2}=$ (500 to 600 cargoes, and a money value of over £1,000,000). These figures give but a vague estimate of the immense business effected in so short a time. Every barrel bearing the "brand" may be bought and sold by local buyers to continental firms on the mere faith of the word "Crown-branded," and that *also without any examination whatever as to the contents of the barrel and the quality of the fish.* It is therefore plainly to be seen that the brand makes business transactions between the buyer and seller comparatively easy. As a contrast, I may state that the unbranded herrings are never bought unless subject to inspection before accepting delivery, or failing that, the seller's guarantee as to quality. Opinions as to quality may differ widely, and therefore contracts for unbrands are not only dangerous but difficult in negotiation. Also, inspection means labour. Labour is money. There is also time lost by seller and buyer. It is clear then that the brand is much to be esteemed, a valuable adjunct, and great facilitator of business, and it is to be hoped that the prestige it has given to the trade may never decline.

For further and more explicit information concerning the brand I would recommend a perusal of the essay on the herring brand—" Fish and Fisheries, 1882."

BENEFICIAL RESULTS — LOCAL TRADE — RAILWAYS — SHIPPING — BANKS — FOREIGN TRADE.

The benefits derived from the Scotch herring fisheries are marvellous in extent and distribution grand in results, and invaluable in wealth. Indirectly the shopkeepers of whatever nature in the herring districts are more or less influenced by its prosperity and continuance. In turn the merchants and manufacturers are benefited through the shops. An extensive and extending business means steady employment for manual labour, and by the necessity of supply so does the labourage increase. Directly, we have the fishermen and their families entirely dependent on the results; and labourers, gutters, coopers, builders, wood merchants, salt manufactures, railways, mercantile marine, banking, and in fact every trade and profession is receiving a support from this great industry. It is no exaggeration to say that the herring fishing is the great industry on whose success or decline the greater part of the Scotch east coast, Shetland, and the Hebrides hang their dependence. Any one acquainted with the Scotch coasts cannot fail to appreciate the great value of the herring fishing.

The basket and net manufacturers have a large field for their output. Every year there is a steady and heavy demand for baskets and nets. There are also the wood merchants at home and abroad being greatly benefited through the trade in supplying them with the different woods necessary for the making of barrels, as also the erecting of sheds and stores. Even the wood shavings or refuse find a good market with those curers who have kilns. Multiply the various instruments described under "plant" by 3000, and you will find that the instrument makers have to be exceedingly thankful for the trade. We must not lose sight of the great demand for wooden spades for the fishermen, salt scoops for the gutting women, gutting knives, hammers, nails, &c. Again, there is the tear and wear in the boat, frequently requiring repairs or improvements at the hands of a boat-builder, a replacing of worn-out ropes and sails and all boats' gear. The wood-hoop merchants find a profitable and extensive business. Builders of fishing boats have been kept exceedingly busy during the past ten years. We must take into consideration the great number of people employed by the merchants and manufacturers in the preparing of the articles requisite by their necessary assistance to the carrying on of fishing and fish curing, all of whom by the demand are enabled to earn good wages. Last, but not least, let us glance at the salt trade. The quantity of salt used yearly is about 100,000 tons, and to the salt manufacturers gives a money value of from £55,000 to £60,000, nett, f.o.b., at places of shipment. The principal manufactories are represented at Runcorn or Liverpool, from whose docks the great bulk is shipped. I give this example to show that benefits are not confined locally, but here we have our sister country reaping benefit from the trade.

Railway Companies are greatly benefited by the vast traffic caused by the herring trade during the season. There is the continual carrying of fresh herrings to the English markets; the occasional transfer of barrels, for export, from the smaller fishing districts to Aberbeen or other large centres for steamer shipment; the carriage of supplies of wood from our home merchants; salt occasionally, hoops, plant, and, above all, the great passenger traffic consequent on the temporary but necessary removings of the fishermen and families for the east coast traffic alone. I estimate that the charges made by the railway companies for the carriage of wood, staves, hoops, salt, plant, and of passengers and their luggage and other necessaries, and of fresh and cured herrings, would be at the lowest not less than £75,000.

Shipping has in the herring trade one of its greatest

supports. Calculating that the average export for the past ten years is 600,000 barrels yearly, that would give as from 500 to 600 cargoes yearly. The average freights to the five principal herring-receiving ports on the continent, viz. Hamburg, 1*s.* 8*d.*; Stettin, 2*s.*; Danzig, 2*s.* 2*d.*; Königsberg, 2*s.* 3*d.*; and Libau, 1*s.* 11*d.*—total average 2*s.* per barrel. The total export for 1882 is given as 782,290¼ barrels, and therefore the gross freights would realise at the 2*s.* freight, £78,229 1*s.* A significant fact, showing the great importance attached to the herring trade by those interested in shipping, is to be found in the marvellous rapidly increasing building of superior steamers especially adapted for the carrying of herrings. Vessels of about 100 tons register are those principally engaged in the trade, and are most suitable.

The banks receive from the fishermen money on deposit at a moderate rate of interest (under 2¾ per cent. for the past few years), and through the great amount of business arising from the trade, and their getting the bank notes put into circulation, thereby receive a great assistance, and derive a considerable profit. I calculate the deposits by the Scotch fishermen to exceed £500,000. As shown in a calculation made later on in this essay, the circulation of notes would be over £1,000,000 yearly. The fish-curers, although turning over a large amount yearly, and thereby being instrumental in the banks' circulation, yet are more generally debtors than creditors of the banks. Their capital is soon absorbed in bounties and stock, and in too many instances they are pretty deep on the wrong side with the bank, but generally such is balanced by heritable or personal security. When the boats are paid off, heavy temporary overdrafts are required. The fish-curer's reputation and character is sufficient to procure that. For some time past the North of Scotland Bank, Limited, has been fully alive to this important industry, and to their credit they have been the means at various centres—notably Fraserburgh—by their monetary assistance to curers, of furthering the development, encouraging its continuance, and of making by its extension a prosperity so plainly discernable. A sufficient compensation is found against the risk in the excellent interest charged by the banks for their accommodations.

The foreign export trade has now assumed an astonishing magnitude. It is not my intention to write regarding the trade in tinned herrings with Australia, or in red herrings with the Mediterranean countries, both of which are of considerable importance, but are comparatively insignificant as compared with the export of pickled herrings to Germany and Russia, of which I endeavour to make a few observations of interest.

In the early part of this century the demand for our herrings in Germany was very limited indeed. For instance, up till 1850 the Danzig market was sufficiently supplied with a yearly import of about 10,000 barrels of Scotch herrings. We must remember, however, that Germany was the great emporium of Norwegian herrings, and it was only on the Scotch cure and catch attaining the supremacy over all other herring fisheries that the demand in Germany increased. For, as the demand and favour for Scotch herrings increased, the prices gradually did the same, and to counterbalance which we have ample evidence that the prices and favour for all other kinds of herrings imported gradually decreased in a corresponding ratio.

There are four great herring centres in Germany, viz. Hamburg, on the Elbe; Stettin, on the Oder; Danzig, on the Vistula; and Königsberg, on the Pregel; and whose imports for 1881 and 1882 are as under:—

	1881.	1882.
Stettin	248,336	267,107
Hamburg	112,349	150,612
Danzig	127,138	142,550
Königsberg	94,308	101,995
Total	582,131	662,264

These figures show that these four centres alone receive about five-sixths of the total exports from Scotland, and the exportation statistics are here given showing the various quantities shipped from the several districts in the respective years:—

	1881. Barrels.	1882. Barrels.
Stornoway	25,038	32,073
Shetland	47,594½	98,292
Orkney	5,990	10,658½
Wick	55,335	73,064
Lobster	17,183	2,912
Helmsdale	15,085	6,330½
Cromarty	746½	2,205½
Findhorn	7,660	3,781½
Buckie	9,360½	9,266½
Banff	25,080	24,131
Fraserburgh	165,362½	178,136½
Peterhead	158,155	156,026½
Aberdeen	83,206½	82,407
Stonehaven	13,723	7,359
Montrose	26,425½	27,662½
Leith	35,138½	46,607
Eyemouth	19,160½	21,377½
Totals for the two years	710,244½	782,290½
		710,244½
Showing an increase for season 1882 of		72,046

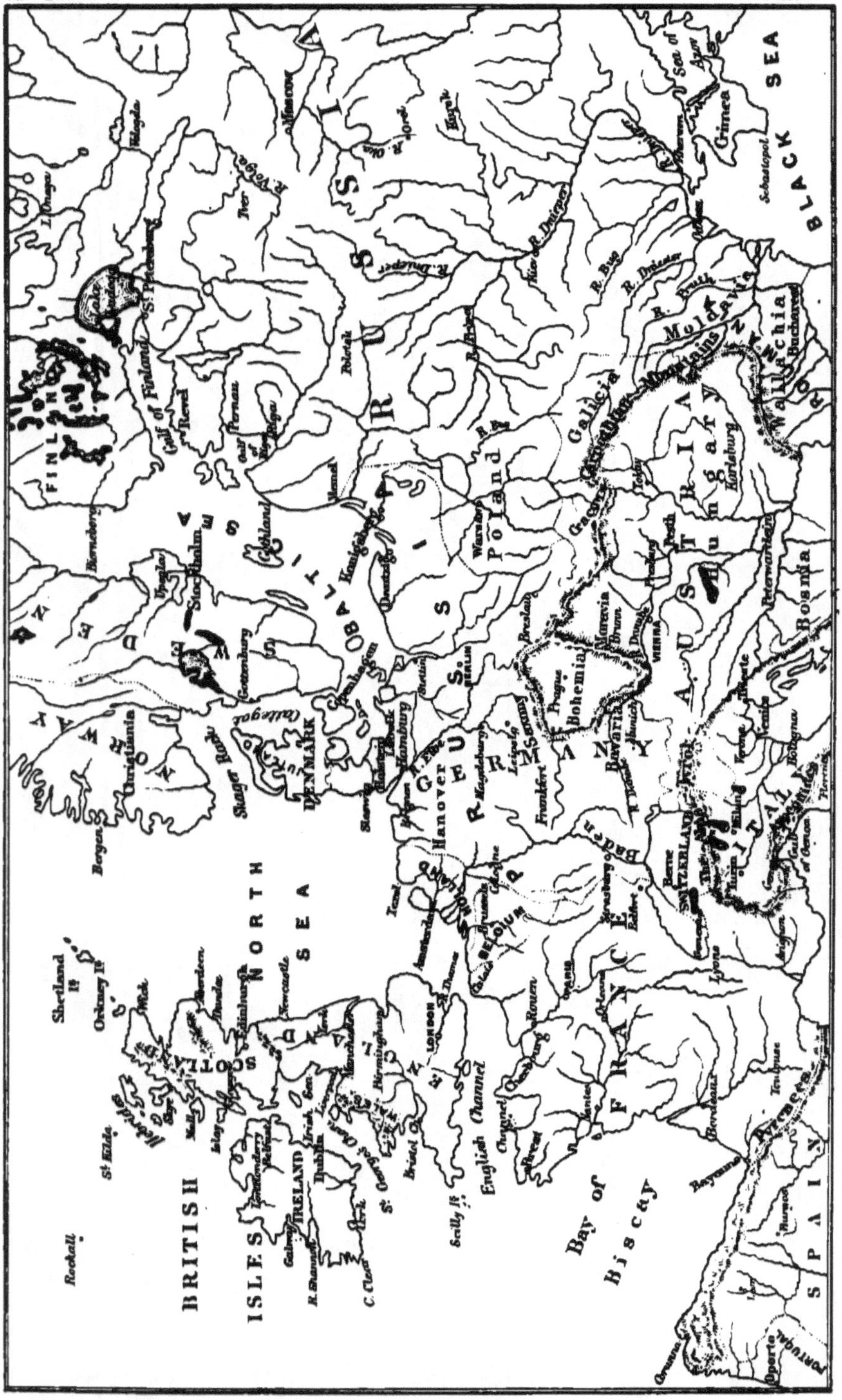
BRITISH ISLES
NORTH SEA
Bay of Biscay
BLACK SEA
English Channel
IRELAND
SCOTLAND
FRANCE
SPAIN
GERMANY
DENMARK
NORWAY
SWEDEN
FINLAND
RUSSIA
BALTIC SEA
AUSTRIA
Hungary
Bohemia
Bavaria
Poland
Galicia
Moldavia
Wallachia
Bosnia
SWITZERLAND
Hanover
Saxony
Baden
Crimea
Shetland Is
Orkney Is
Rockall
St Kilda
LONDON
Dublin
Bristol
Hamburg
Berlin
Prague
Vienna
Bergen
Christiania
Stockholm
Copenhagen
Gulf of Finland
Sea of Azov
Pyrenees
Carpathian Mountains

A few of the other German ports are Harburg, Bremen, Lübeck, Pernau, and Memel, but they do not receive regular supplies. There are also numerous inland towns noted for their extensive transactions in herrings, the principal being Magdeburg, Halle, Leipzig, Breslau, Berlin, Frankfurt, Posen, and others of lesser note too numerous to mention. Russia seems to give a preference to Norwegian and Swedish herrings, the duty on which is much lighter than that on the Scotch. The duty on Scotch herrings is by far too heavy. Nevertheless, Scotch herrings to a limited extent command good prices through such markets as Libau, Riga, and St. Petersburg. These three Russian centres have a fair share of our west coast herrings, but they only receive a stray cargo now and then from the east coast. West coast and east coast early herrings, from their oily tendency, are in much demand at medium prices, but between the excessive charges and duty to be paid, the Russian people cannot afford to pay high prices. If the duty could be reduced to about level with the German, then an extended business would be the result; in the meantime the Russian prices and currency are of so fluctuating a character, that our curers and buyers must be cautious in the trade with Russia. However, Libau is strengthening its connection with us, and proving a great rival to its German neighbouring centre—Königsberg. Odessa, in the Black Sea, has lately been doing a direct business—principally through London agents—and it is hoped that such business will rapidly extend itself in the future. A glance at the accompanying map will show the situations of the centres I have referred to, and how admirably they command the interior business throughout Germany, Austria, and Russia.

CONCLUSION—HISTORY AND LEGISLATURE—STATISTICS SHOWING PROSPERITY AND WEALTH—MUCH REQUIRED AND EXPECTED IMPROVEMENTS REFERRED TO.

There is very little authentic imformation to be had regarding the Scotch herring fisheries before the sixteenth century. Having gradually risen from obscurity by slow but steady degrees, it was then in importance in close rivalry with the Dutch. There is mention made of the fishings as early as the 13th and 14th centuries, and as in the 15th century it must have left its mark on some of the old records of that time, surely, by diligent searching, some information might be got at once interesting and valuable.

From 1630 to 1650 a further impetus was given to its prosecution, was successful, and apparently every year proved a steady increase. In 1676, a reaction set in, and its downward career was swift. The companies then in vogue were utterly quashed. However, private enterprise was quietly persevering, and thanks thereto, the herring fishing had by the end of the century actually got ahead of the Dutch.

From 1695 to 1707 success attended the enterprise and efforts of improvement. But the next seven years again saw a retrograde period, and the fishing nearly ceased altogether. This probably principal national industry was, by the stupid and complicated regulations and laws of the Legislature immediately after the union, nearly suppressed, and that at a time when its supremacy over other nations was most promising. In the years 1714, 1720, 1727, 1750, bold attempts were made to revive the trade. Large companies were again established, backed up and assisted by the Government, but the expected great results were never realised. A better year happened to be 1757, and the fishings kept steady thereafter till 1767, after which came the periodical backwardness, culminating in 1782, when we read the total catch was only 12,522 barrels for that year. The legislation of 1808, on fishery laws and regulations, laid the foundation of all its future workings, and it is from this period that we have a continual and progressive success. Several excellent alterations and additions were made by the Act 55, Geo. III. 694, 14th June 1815, and about this time the east coast seemed to be endowed with a new life. Herring curing seemed prosperous, and the small coast villages in many cases in a few years grew into fair-sized and prosperous towns. Perhaps the best example is Fraserburgh. Twenty years ago an insignificant 'Burgh indeed, but at this day the Scotch herring capital. Built on and around Kinnaird Head, it has the command of the Moray Firth. To the south lies its beautiful bay. Jutting out from the Kinnaird Castle is the breakwater, extending south and at the middle south-east, and shelters the harbours and the bay. It is 810 yards in length, and its average thickness about 30 feet. At its point there is a good lighthouse. The Balaklava Harbour at Fraserburgh is the largest herring boat harbour on the coast. It is $12\frac{3}{4}$ acres in extent.

The growing importance of the herring fishing has caused several inquiries and commissions to take place, and the results have always tended to its well-being. I refer to such years as 1832, 1843, 1852, 1859, and the more modern but the most important of 1881.

The following statistics show the total catch of herrings

for the past twenty-six years, for the entire east coast including Shetland, Lewis, and Barra, viz. for—

1857 . . . 329,251 crans.	1869 . . . 403,633 crans.
1858 . . . 393,035 ,,	1870 . . . 596,421 ,,
1859 . . . 302,943 ,,	1871 . . . 562,865 ,,
1860 . . . 463,100 ,,	1872 . . . 562,737 ,,
1861 . . . 485,645 ,,	1873 . . . 714,717 ,,
1862 . . . 520,280 ,,	1874 . . . 720,964 ,,
1863 . . . 439,210 ,,	1875 . . . 655,606 ,,
1864 . . . 432,064 ,,	1876 . . . 406,440 ,,
1865 . . . 395,157 ,,	1877 . . . 561,439 ,,
1866 . . . 413,065 ,,	1878 . . . 618,597 ,,
1867 . . . 474,098 ,,	1879 . . . 516,406 ,,
1868 . . . 366,068 ,,	1880 . . . 930,307 ,,

	1881. Crans.	1882. Crans.
Stornoway	41,950	45,980
Shetland	46,500	102,250
Orkney	14,418	16,018
Wick	61,742	81,792
Lybster	16,688	1,730
Helmsdale	16,388	6,404
Cromarty	1,638	1,376
Findhorn	6,890	4,872
Buckie	7,173	7,630
Banff	22,106	23,003
Fraserburgh	132,642	139,451
Peterhead	124,878	124,185
Aberdeen	78,702	80,363
Stonehaven	19,355	15,910
Montrose	26,012	28,820
Leith	7,216	3,660
Eyemouth	59,486	59,825
	683,784	743,269
Deduct season 1881		683,784
Showing an increase for season 1882 of		59,485

And for the past five years the total catch at the individual stations :—

Stations and Districts.	1878.	1879.	1880.	1881.	1882.
WICK	84,248	63,094	113,186	55,542	69,926
Lybster and Clyth	6,910	9,240	12,371	15,231	1,626
Forse	282	620	592	219	28
Latheronwheel	512	790	637	1,237	78
Dunbeath	1,502	2,800	1,056	1,802	504
Helmsdale	7,600	10,855	10,285	13,783	3,920
Portmahomack	858	1,391	1,790	1,515	1,376
Burghead and Hopeman	1,122	3,009	5,200	3,090	2,328
Lossiemouth	819	4,896	7,600	3,800	2,544
Buckie District	2,864	3,832	12,413	7,173	7,630
Portsoy	4,935	4,670	6,950	5,600	4,650
Whitehills	1,102	1,610	1,667	840	1,174
Banff	250	1,360	1,913	1,606	3,030
Macduff	4,756	7,384	8,530	5,538	9,762
Gardenstown	4,058	7,007	6,915	7,685	4,387
Fraserburgh	175,820	105,037	218,504	132,613	139,500
Peterhead	122,456	83,200	177,300	124,800	124,185
Aberdeen	69,231	36,400	78,810	78,657	80,253
Stonehaven	..	..	..	..	15,910
Montrose District	26,758	30,048	54,091	45,352	28,820
Anstruther „	3,975	6,490	7,840	3,660	3,145
Leith to Dunbar	1,500	5,460	4,600	4,110	2,722
Eyemouth District	25,407	52,149	48,715	59,486	59,825
Orkney	14,722	8,364	16,142	14,418	16,160
Shetland	6,240	6,700	38,700	46,250	102,000
Lewis and Bárra	50,670	60,000	94,500	41,100	45,240

Stonehaven has been this year disjoined from the Montrose district, and erected into a separate station. In the foregoing tables we therefore give the results for 1882 separately, although for the previous years they are all included in the Montrose district.

A perusal of the foregoing statistics will prove that although yearly fluctuations have taken place, yet that every periodical decade proves that the prosperity as regards the catch is steadily on the increase. The quality and selection have also much improved, thanks to wise regulations and our national characteristic intrepidity. The prices also are year by year becoming more firm, are less speculative, fluctuate less than in former years, and are now entirely regulated according to supply and demand. The supply, apparently always increasing, is at the present moment very great, but it is pleasing to state that the demand is proportionally quite as great and strong.

In recapitulation, the following calculations are here given to show the reader some idea as to the wealth of the herring trade.

CAPITAL.

	£
Fishermen's boats, all necessary gear included—	
6131 boats at £275 per boat	1,686,025
6131 boats' "fleets" of nets at 70s. per net, allowing 25 nets to each boat	536,432
Fish-curer's invested capital, lowest estimate	720,000
Total	£2,942,457

ONE YEAR'S BUSINESS (1882).

	£	s.
Bounties paid to fishermen—		
6131 boats at £40 per boat	245,240	0
Prices paid to fishermen for herrings—		
743,269 crans at average of 18s. per cran	668,942	2
167 new boats, with all necessary gear, at £310 per boat	51,770	0
167 new "fleets" of nets—30 per boat, at 70s. per net	17,535	0
For new nets distributed amongst the fleet	15,000	0
Lowest estimate for repairs on the fleet (paid to boat-builders, rope and sail makers, block and tackle manufacturers, Cutch dealers, &c.)	12,500	0
Total paid "to" and "by" fishermen	£1,010,987	2

Fish-curer's outlay, interest on capital, rent of yard, plant, stock and work, wages to coopers, gutters, labourers, cartage, shore dues. Equal to about 8*s.* 6*d.* per barrel £394,862

Fish-curer's income—return for herrings—
743,269 crans = 929,086 barrels at 30*s.* per barrel £1,393,628

We must not forget that the fishermen own seven-eighths of the houses they inhabit, and also, that they are heavy depositors with our Scotch banks. Many of the fish-curers are affluent, and possess both money and property. Likewise, the Scotch buyers for foreign export, who may be said to turn over once more the great money circulation of this trade.

Of the much required and expected improvements, it is apparent that harbour accommodation is the most needed. It is gratifying to note that the surplus branding fees are to be devoted in that improvement, and that a large Government grant may be shortly expected for an east coast harbour of refuge. Whilst large centres are receiving every assistance, even at present, there are small centres who receive little or none. Some are most deserving, and ready to spring into a new energetic life whenever they get a new harbour, or an extension.

With a rapidity quite amazing, the improvements in our boats, gear, and nets, have sprung into force within the past dozen of years. The herring fishing is year by year being prosecuted further from the shore, and large and finer sea-going boats are becoming necessary. If such continues, to prevent the quality of the fish retrograding, the application of steam to our fishing boats will be necessary. Already I can see symptoms of an east coast steamboat herring fishing.

Last, but not least, comes the great necessity for improving the social condition of our fishermen, and especially of providing suitable and proper accommodation for them at the herring centres. I sincerely hope that circumstances may arise at an early date that will demand an inquiry, the result of which will tend to the much needed rectification of a backward mode of living. A very slight monetary expenditure and a few forcible regulations are all that is requisite to right this matter. The success of the trade is due in a great measure to the fishermen and their steady enterprise, but they have nearly gone as far as they can; at least, it is not their business to provide temporary residences at every place they may go to fish. It must therefore lie with the curers (employers), or through Government agency to provide the needful. Our fishing is progressive, so let us hope that our fishermen will also be so. Progress the watchword, and Prosperity the result.

International Fisheries Exhibition
LONDON, 1883

MACKEREL AND PILCHARD FISHERIES

BY

THOMAS CORNISH

LONDON
WILLIAM CLOWES AND SONS, LIMITED
INTERNATIONAL FISHERIES EXHIBITION
AND 13 CHARING CROSS, S.W.
1883

LONDON:
PRINTED BY WILLIAM CLOWES AND SONS, Limited,
STAMFORD STREET AND CHARING CROSS.

International Fisheries Exhibition
LONDON, 1883

CONFERENCE ON 13TH JULY, 1883.

Sir JOHN ST. AUBYN, Bart., M.P., in the Chair.

THE CHAIRMAN, in introducing Mr. Cornish, said he had come at the request of the Executive Committee to tell them something about a subject on which most people knew comparatively little. Whilst almost everybody in the room was more or less intimately acquainted with the mackerel, there were very few, except those who lived in Cornwall, on the west coast of Ireland, and on the coast of Brittany, who knew anything about the pilchard; but they might take it on his authority that the pilchard was a most excellent fish when eaten fresh, and when preserved, either after the manner of sardines in oil, or salted for exportation, it formed a most nutritious and excellent article of diet. The Cornish fishermen were employed to a very large extent both in the mackerel and pilchard fisheries, and went out a considerable distance from the shore in quest of these fish. They met with the mackerel at spring-time at a distance varying from close in-shore, to sixty, seventy, or one hundred miles out, and twenty-four hours after they were caught, people in London were in a position to judge of the result by seeing the mackerel on the slabs of fishmongers. A pilchard was a different sort of fish altogether. It did not readily bear carriage, but had to be eaten as soon as possible after it was out of the water, and consequently the great trade in pilchards was when they were salted or preserved in oil. He could not give the statistics of the men, boats, and capital employed, but, to give some idea of the magnitude of the fisheries, he might mention that, in his own immediate neighbourhood, the water on which he could look down from his own windows contained within two and a half miles a fleet of something like four hundred boats, with all kinds of nets and gear and other appliances, representing a capital of something like £140,000. If a proportional amount of capital and men were employed in other parts of the country, it could readily be seen how important those fisheries were. They were not only important as a means of providing food, but formed an excellent nursery and school for a race of seamen than whom there were none, either in this kingdom or anywhere else in Europe, more industrious, steady, independent or courageous.

MACKEREL AND PILCHARD FISHERIES.

LADIES AND GENTLEMEN,—The honour has been done me of requesting me to read a Paper before you on the "Mackerel and the Pilchard," and I presume that this has been done, because I come from West Cornwall, the principal English home of the fisheries for these two fish, and am well acquainted with them; but my ignorance makes it advisable that I should confine my remarks to the familiar facts which I know of these fish in my own county, rather than attempt to deal with the subject scientifically.

The mackerel is the head, or typical fish, but one of the smallest in size, of a large family, which has representatives in every sea in the world, except in the regions of extreme cold, and every member of which is excellent as food.

The first distinguishing mark of the family to an outside observer is a tail having a peculiar fork. You can see it in a moment in the fish market here. The next is the cleanness of the lines on which the fish is built. The long conical forepart of the body and snout, the smooth round body, and the clean run of the afterpart, all fit the fish for rapid propulsion through the water, whilst the powerful forked tail, working with much less opposition to the water than would a rounded tail, and precisely with the action with which the sailor sculls his boat by one oar over the stern, enables the fish to make the greatest possible use of the advantages of its shape. The last distinguishing exterior feature which I shall notice is the existence between the base of the tail fin, and the hindmost upper and under fins, and both above and below the body, of a series of little soft rudimentary fins, called finlets, and the use of which is obscure. This family includes the bonitos, the tunnies, the albacores, and other Mediterranean fish, all occasional visitants of our Western seas, and just excludes (if, indeed, it does exclude, for I, who have seen the fish, am not clear about it,) the Northern "opah," a noble great fellow, some four to five feet long, which would more than cover an ordinary card-table, and is a very Assyrian for "gleaming in purple and gold," being in fact almost the only northern fish which excels in splendour of colour the fish of the seas of the temperate zones and the tropics. I do not at this moment recollect whether there is a specimen of this fish in the building. If there is, you will find it in the court of Norway or possibly of Denmark.

But, of all the family, the mackerel is the most fitted for rapid propulsion and has the most powerful tail; and this, you know, means the greatest power of propulsion, for the sole natural propulsive power of every fish lies in its tail. I once proved this beyond question, thus :—We stay in summer in a house so close to the sea that we are in our boat within a minute of our leaving our front door, and we have there a pill, or salt water pool, in the rocks, about thirty feet long by ten wide by three deep, which is left by the tide for about six hours in every tide, and into this pool we put the fish which we bring in alive from our trammels every morning, and watch them until we want them.

I have watched an octopus in that pool many times. But once I cut off the tail of a fish, a pollock I think, and I put it in this pool. At first the fish did not realise its loss, and we saw the stump of its tail working, but the other fins were, as usual, only balancing the fish. There was no progression. After a while the fish stopped working the stump of the tail, and lay simply balanced. About an hour afterwards I came back to it, and it was slowly progressing by using its pectoral fins (those next behind the gills) as oars. I had seen all I wanted to know, and had ascertained that the tail fin was the fin of propulsion, that the fish had sense enough to find out when it had lost it, and reason enough to adapt its pectoral fins to a use for which they were never intended. I then killed the fish, but my conscience did not, nor does it, accuse me of any cruelty towards it. It showed no symptoms of pain. Indeed, of all the very many thousands of fish that I have seen die, I never saw one show symptoms of pain. The nearest approach to it has occurred in the crimping of skate immediately on its being taken out of the water. The crimping is done by drawing a sharp knife in three cuts to the bone, on each side of and parallel to the back-bone. The fish writhes under the knife, but from muscular action, I think, more than from pain, and before the last cut is given it is dead. And this, in my opinion, is a much more merciful way of dealing with the skate, than allowing it to lie suffocating in the bottom of your boat for the hour which it occupies in dying that way. I know many good people say that we should kill our fish as we catch them. If we could, we would, for they would be so much the better for the table, but in most kinds of sea fishing this is utterly impossible. Take a mackerel seine for instance. A tolerably successful haul ought to produce at least 2,000 fish. After the haul commences, everything depends on the speed with which it is completed. Every hand on board the boat is at it, and in a few minutes the 2,000 fish are spluttering about in the bottom of the boat. I once took upwards of 6 cwt. of fish, principally skate, on a long line of 500 hooks (i.e. 500 fathoms) stretched along the bottom of the sea in shallow water, in one haul. The whole hauling had to be done with the least possible stoppage, and at times the fish came so fast, that the boatmen attending on me had not time to unhook them, and had to cut away the snoodings. The fish had to lie in the bottom of the boat and die, we could not stop to kill them. And in the end I found that the line had cut my two forefingers almost to the bone. The fish were crueller to me that day than I was to the fish.

Whether viewed for its colour or its form, the mackerel is one of the most beautiful of English fish. I need not describe it to you. Doubtless its form is familiar to you all. And if it is not you have only to go into the fish-market here and see it in as much perfection as it can retain after a long journey. Beautiful as the mackerel on a London fishmonger's stall is, much more beautiful is it as it comes out of the water alive. There is, in the best mackerel, an iridescent, rosy tint under the gills and forepart of the body, which I have seen in fish here, but which is much more conspicuous when they are taken. And it is this colour by which our fishermen judge their fish. They say, "*Red* mackerel is *good* mackerel; *white* mackerel is mackerel; *green* mackerel is poison."

And in this last remark they are quite correct. Whenever a green hue supersedes the rosy, the flesh of the fish when eaten will, with very many people, produce most unpleasant symptoms of blood poisoning; and as these green mackerel are taken amongst the others at all times of the year, they give the fish a bad name, and cause people to abuse the whole family, when the truth is that they ought to have made a better selection.

An average mackerel weighs $1\frac{1}{2}$ lbs., which gives about 1,500 fish to the ton. Large fish go to 2 lbs. or even $2\frac{1}{2}$ lbs. but they are rare, and as they do not sell for more than the others, are reserved by the fishermen for presents to their friends, which starts another of our West Cornwall notions that "you should never eat a mackerel unless it is given to you." This saying is quite understood in West Cornwall now, but in process of time it will very probably get to be understood there, as meaning that it is unlucky to *buy* mackerel, and if that belief once gets about, well, we are a superstitious people, and you ladies and gentlemen in London will have a large addition to your supply of that fish from Cornwall.

These large mackerel are usually females, with roes ready to be shed, and are known as *Queen* mackerel and *King* mackerel, but I do not recollect ever seeing a large male mackerel of this sort.

Sometimes one is startled by an announcement in the

papers that a mackerel of six or even eight pounds weight has been caught, but in every instance in which I have been able to make inquiries the fish has turned out to belong to an allied species—the short finned tunny—which sometimes herds with the mackerel.

There is one fact about the personal history of this fish, which I will mention although I know I do it at the risk of having my veracity suspected; but I narrate only what I have seen over and over again, have repeatedly shown to my friends, and am prepared to show in the cases of two fish out of three, to any one of you who will call on me at Penzance and go out and catch mackerel with me. The mackerel, like the turbot, requires, and has, enormous muscular power at the tail to give the tail-fin its full advantages. In the turbot the fishermen recognise this fact and say that the turbot has a "second heart," and, as soon as they can, after they have caught one, they, at least in our parts, "bleed it," that is, make an incision on the line of the lateral line on the white near the tail, which cuts into this "second heart," and from which the fish bleeds freely. They have an impression that it whitens the white. Now, for my mackerel. The strongest and most muscular fish are those which wander about by themselves, and take surface bait, and it is on these only that my experiment has been tried. Take one of these immediately it comes into your boat, and, at once, without injuring it more than is necessary, prepare it for the gridiron just as your cook would, and lay it on the deck of the boat. In a short time a muscular action will develop itself in the tail, and the disembowelled fish will turn a clear summersault, sometimes two, and occasionally three, and will then become quiet after a convulsion in which every fin vibrates. Like many other discoveries this one was made by accident; but I call your attention to the fact that very much the same sort of thing happens in the case of a common snake killed, and dead beyond all question, but in which a muscular action goes on for hours, and gives rise to the common idea that a snake never dies until sunset. And I think our medical men can tell us that a very strong muscular action occasionally takes place in the human body after death from some particular convulsive diseases.

Taking the season through, a mackerel is worth two pence at the boat's side, and, with that fact before you, I leave you to judge how much the railway carrier and the fishmonger between them get out of the consumer.

Of course the price varies from day to day. Within the last month I have known mackerel selling at the boat's side for two and six pence per one hundred and twenty, or just one farthing per fish; and a boat with a catch of eight hundred threw them all overboard rather than come into harbour and pay her quay dues. On the other hand I have seen them selling at the boat's side at one shilling per fish.

The mackerel fishery of Cornwall is a very old one. The fish itself was known in our seas very long ago, for it has a name in the old Cornish language ("brithel"), but it was but a small affair until railways opened up our markets in 1859. I find that in 1808 we were sending mackerel from Penzance to Portsmouth in sailing cutters, but the record does not say in what condition they arrived there. It was probably fortunate for their owners that there were no Sanitary Inspectors about the markets in those days.

At this time, the fleet employed on the fishery in Cornwall consists of about 400 sails of luggers of about 15 to 18 tons burden, excellent sea-boats (of which many models are to be seen on the Cornwall stall in the British Fisheries Gallery), costing, when the nets are on board, six hundred pounds each. They are capable of going closer to the wind than any ordinary yacht. The spread of canvas they make is, as you can see for yourselves, enormous, and they will live in exceedingly heavy weather; but they give in sometimes. Three years ago the boat *Jane* succumbed to a fearful cross sea, and sank within two hundred yards (one hundred fathoms) of Penzance pierhead, and drowned her crew of six men and a boy, not only within sight of their own homes, but within sight of their wives and children, who knew what boat she was. But even in that case, the men who knew said she was lost because she had not sufficient canvas on her to force her through the sea.

If one of these boats is overpowered by the sea, she takes down her spars and makes them and her nets and such of her sails as she can afford to risk into a kind of raft, under the slight shelter of which she rides out the gale; but you will find on the "Cornwall Stall" a suggestion for a very great improvement in this method. The exhibitor is a Cornishman, and he calls it a "floating anchor." It consists of a beam of timber to which is attached a large square piece of canvas, to which is attached another beam of timber from which there trails away a perforated zinc can which finds its place, when at work, in the cavity of a cone made of canvas, fastened to a wooden hoop. When the boat is storm-pressed she lowers her masts, heads up to wind, and hoists the whole machine out ahead of her and makes fast to the first beam; and then, being deeper in the water than the machine, she drifts astern and down the wind towing the anchor, the outer beam of the anchor stretches the canvas sheet, and is assisted in doing this by the cone which it is dragging mouth foremost. The cone meanwhile is receiving from the zinc can, oil which exudes from it, and which the cone itself sends out in a fan shape. Thus, an advancing wave first meets the oil, of the effect of which we have heard so much lately. It then meets, and perhaps breaks against the forward beam, and then has to pass under or fall on the sheet and in any case will reach the boat in a very enfeebled condition. I find practical men are speaking very well of this invention.

Each of our boats carries a crew of seven men and a boy (the latter usually a relative of one of the crew), and is owned by a practical fisherman—very frequently by the master or his father—and is worked on the share system, under which each man brings a certain number of nets on board, and the proceeds of each season are shared in a peculiar and complicated way between the boats, the crew, and the nets. We have no large boat-owners and no boat-owning companies. This state of affairs produces results which, like many other things in Cornwall, are peculiar to the county. When the Commissioners came down last year on the inquiry as to—

>Cruelty to fisherboys.
>
>The prevention of desertion, and
>
>The method of paying wages.

we satisfied them that under our system there was, in our fisheries :—

>No cruelty to fisherboys.
>
>No desertion—self-interest preventing it.
>
>No disputes as to wages.

This last thing puzzled the Commissioners most of all. After the meeting two fishermen and myself were standing in the lobby when the Chairman came to us and said :—

"I am satisfied you have no disputes about wages, but I cannot make out how it is done." And I turned to one of the fishermen and said, "Tell the gentleman how it is done," and he said, "We leave all that to the women."

It will be seen from the numbers which I have given, that our mackerel fishery gives employment to about 3,000 men and boys, who, between the month of February when the season begins and June when it ends, usually catch about 4,000 tons of fish, which will give six millions of individuals. As soon as our mackerel season is over the pilchard season begins, and when it ends, our fleet sails for the Irish fishery, the Plymouth fishery, or the East coast of England fisheries; for they can go anywhere. One once reached Australia safely, but now, in these days when 14 foot punts cross the Atlantic, that is no great feat.

Still, in 1854, when the *Mystery*, of 36 foot keel and about 15 tons burden made her voyage, no boat of her size had ever attempted to deal with the Atlantic Ocean since the Caravel, which was the smallest of the little fleet of Columbus, had done so 350 years before, and she was in company with large vessels, and therefore the voyage of the *Mystery* remains noteworthy. This solitary boat sailed from Mount's Bay on the 18th November, 1854, and reached Melbourne on the 14th March, 1855, after a voyage of 117 days. She had a crew of seven men and carried her nets. I have recovered the log which was kept on board of her,* and, judging from it, a more dreary voyage than hers was never made. Beyond sighting a few ships and a few albatrosses, and being fêted at Table Bay, nothing seems to have occurred of more importance than "the broaching of the second barrel of pork," until they were nearing Australia, and then, for a short time, things got exciting, and they met with weather which made them ride

* Kindly lent to me by Mrs. Boase, the widow of the seaman who kept it.

to a raft in the way which I have described, and which they describe.

Thus, on 18th February, 1855, the Log says :—

Sunday, February 18th, 1855.

Lat. by acct. 40° 5′ S.; Long. 81° 25′ E.

A.M. Strong gales with heavy sea running.

4 A.M. Gale still increasing, handed the foresail and set a reef second mizzen forward.

6 „ Terrific gale with a tremendous heavy sea running, and carried away the second mizzen yard. Brought the ship head to wind and hove a raft out.

6·30 A.M. Split the third mizzen, unbent it, and bent the new one.

8 „ Gale still increasing, with more sea and heavy rain.

NOON. Ditto, weather.

3 P.M. Less wind and sea, made sail, set reef second mizzen forward.

MIDNIGHT. Strong squally weather.

Friday, February 23rd, 1855.

2 P.M. Gale fast increasing.

4 „ A complete hurricane, with mountains of sea and very heavy rain. Brought the ship head to wind. Ship riding very easy to a raft prepared for the purpose.

7 „ Rather less wind. Veering to the westward, hauled the raft on board, made sail, set reef second mizzen forward.

Saturday, February 24th, 1855.

A.M. Strong winds with a heavy sea on.

4 „ Moderating, set storm foresail and jib; squared.

8 P.M. Light airs and cloudy, all possible sail set.

10 „ Heavy rain. Wind inclined northerly.

NOON. Jibed ship. Lat. by acct. 40° S.; Long. by acct. 101° E.

P.M. Wind veering all round the compass, with heavy showers of snow and sleet.

3 P.M. Set the jib.

4 „ More wind, took in the large sails and set storm foresail and third mizzen.

5 „ Heavy gusts of wind and rain, ship running under bare poles.

6 „ Set reef second mizzen forward.

7 „ Very heavy squalls. Hauled down second mizzen.

8 „ Set second mizzen.

10 „ Down sail.

11 „ Set it again.

MIDNIGHT. Very strong squally weather.

Monday, March 5th, 1855.

AM. Strong gale, with mountains of sea. Ship running under reef second mizzen forward. Shipping a great quantity of water on deck.

4 P.M. Gale increasing with a great deal more sea.

6 P.M. Complete hurricane. Brought the ship head to wind, riding very easy, raft prepared for the purpose.

MIDNIGHT. Very heavy weather, with a high sea running.

Tuesday, 6th March, 1855.

A.M. A terrific gale of wind, it being the heaviest that we have experienced since leaving England. Our gallant little boat rides the mountains of sea remarkably well, not shipping any water whatever, having dry decks fore and aft. I am confident that she is making better weather at present than a great many ships would if here.

4 A.M. Heavy gust of wind.
8 ,, More moderate.
9 ,, Hauled the raft on board, made sail, set reef second mizzen forward.
NOON. Very strong weather. Lat. by observation, 40° S. Long. by chronometer, 131° E.

Saturday, 10th March, 1855.

A.M. Very heavy gale with a high sea running, ship riding very easy to a raft.
8 A.M. Ditto Weather; repairing the second mizzen.
NOON. Rather less wind and sea. Lat. by observation, 38° 39′ S.; Long. by chronometer, 140° 45′ E.
6 P.M. Hauled the raft on board; made sail, set storm sails.
10 ,, Moderating fast.
11 ,, Made the Australian land between Cape Northumberland and Cape Bridgwater. Tacked ship. Wind off the shore.
MIDNIGHT. Very fine weather.

The log does not state her rate of sailing, but I learn from Mr. J. C. James, who is related to one of the crew, that during one period of twenty-four consecutive hours she made eight knots, which is the equivalent of something like nine and a half miles per hour.

Our men, when on the home mackerel fishery, sell their fish to buyers—who are sent down by the large London and other houses for the purpose—in a very primitive but very effective fashion. The auctioneer takes his station on the beach in the early morning with the buyers around him.

A boat appears in the offing, and signals her number and the number of fish she has. The auctioneer announces both, and, if the bidding is slack, chucks a stone into the air. The buyers have to bid before that stone falls. If a bid comes, another stone is chucked up, and so on. And as the boats do not all arrive at the same time, this method conduces to much speculation.

Sometimes the fleet puts into Scilly, and sends the catch to the mainland by steamer. Then the market is steadier, because the total of the catch is known by telegraph; but scenes of wild excitement take place. The early boats unload and pack their fish and stow the baskets on board the steamer, but the late boats crowd round the steamer, which is a mail boat and bound to time, and simply unload their fish on to her decks. These fish are packed on the way over by men working against time. I came over in the steamer once when she had more than 60,000 fish on board, and I watched the packing of more than 15,000 of them, which had been thrown loose upon her deck, after which I considered I could say that I knew mackerel when I saw it. It was on a hot summer's day, and as the steamer rolled to the Land's End seas, the packers were constantly ankle-deep in blood and slush.

One result of this investigation was the certain conclusion that the "scribbled mackerel" and "dotted mackerel" of Couch (British Fishes) were only accidental varieties of the common mackerel.

Strictly speaking the mackerel is not a migratory fish. It is in our seas all the year round, but in the season which I have mentioned—February to June—it, for some unknown purpose, crowds from the deep sea inshore. By day, during this season, it swims in scools or shoals, and by night it makes a formation in loose order, probably for the purpose of feeding; but it never pursues, as true migrants do, any settled route. The fishermen have to search for their fish day by day. In the day-time the fish are taken by the scool or shoal in shallow water by the seine net, a net shot ahead of and around them. In the night-time they are taken by the drift-net, a net shot over the boat's side, and fastened at one end to the drifting boat, which goes with the wind or tide or both as may happen. The fleet represents a capital of about £240,000, the property of *bonâ fide* fishermen, and certainly deserves the protection which it requires. The drifters are much put upon by trawlers. These latter drive in hours which belong to the former. Trawling is a day fishery; driving is a night fishery, and every now and then the slow moving, helpless, illegally fishing trawler comes across the nets of the equally helpless but legally fishing driver and carries them away. This happens in the night time; the driver never has a punt with her and cannot ascertain the trawler's number. In fact she does not know that the mischief is done until she hauls her nets, and she has no remedy. I have known £400 of damage done to the drivers in this way in a single week. The thing could be easily prevented; a gunboat or even a Government cutter cruising on the fishing-ground during the two months in Spring in which the ·mischief happens, would stop the whole thing. Some years since we had reasons for expecting to see that gunboat come round the Lizard every day for three seasons in succession, but she never came, and we gave up expecting her.

There is another matter in connection with our Mount's Bay fleet, and I believe it affects also some of the other fleets, which I think may interest you. Just before the *Jane*, of which I spoke just now, was lost, a Mutual Fishing Boat Insurance Club was started for the Mount's

Bay fleet. But we had then lost no boats lately, and our men were indifferent about it, and the thing fell flat. Only seven boats were entered in it. It happened that the *Jane*, and two other boats, partially wrecked in the same storm, were in it, and the club was ruined. The public generously gave us over £2,000 to provide for the widows and orphans of the crew of the *Jane*, and to repair damages generally. Out of this fund we provided liberally for the widows and orphans, and we then paid to the club enough to enable it to meet the demands on it, and we then distributed the remainder of the fund amongst the other owners whose boats had sustained damage, with the distinct assurance that if they did not put their boats in the club no one would ever again stir a finger to help them in case of accident. The Cornish fisherman is not behindhand in taking a hint, and I believe every boat in the bay is now in the club, even before she is launched. I certainly do not wish to see any club make its prosperity by such a fearful experience as that which set up ours, but I shall be most happy to send the rules of the club to any one interested in the matter. The general outline is just this: nets are not insurable (for want of that gunboat.) The surveyor of the club examines each boat entered and reports on her value, and she is then insured in two-thirds of her survey value. Losses are made good by the levy of a rate on all owners of boats in the club at the time of the loss, and no loss is made good which is occasioned by any neglect to observe the Board of Trade Rules.

I wish to call your attention to a great advantage which this Exhibition will certainly confer on Cornwall. Mackerel shoal in deep water as well as in shallow. Our desideratum for a long time past has been a seine which can capture the deep water shoals. A gentleman named Cox, a Cornishman, has invented a seine of which a model is in the middle of our Cornwall stall (it is the one which has the weight attached to it), which he says can be worked at deep sea shoals of fish; and curiously enough, a model of a second seine on the same principle, but differing a little in detail, is exhibited on the same stall by Mr. Moses Dunn, of Fowey, and a third by Mr. Barron of Mevagissey. Practical men saw these models, both before they came here and since, and pronounced them very pretty little toys, which might succeed in a fish pond, but utterly unfit for use at sea. Now a full seine costs a large sum of money, and no hard-headed capitalist is likely to lay it out on a speculation which the practical men tell him must fail. Well, the nets come here, and to them came an American gentleman and he said, "You have the precise principle on which we are working deep-sea seines in America, and they succeed admirably."

There is another point which I must not overlook. There is an idea of great antiquity, and very generally entertained, that mackerel must always be fresh to be good. It is perfectly true that mackerel is in its perfection when cooked as soon as captured, but if that cannot be done it is like most other fish, none the worse for a little keeping. And it is for this reason, and because ice takes the flavour out of the fish, that I consider dry packing (ie., packing fish-upon-fish without ice) preferable to packing in ice; it injures the flavour less. But there is another view to be taken. This fish is eminently amenable to the action of antiseptics. The smallness and fineness of its scale causes an antiseptic bath to act upon its skin and gilled surfaces with marked effect. I once received two of the large mackerel of which I have spoken, which had been caught off the Scilly Isles on a Monday night in the month of June (I believe, at all events in the height of summer); I received them in their natural state on Tuesday evening, and put them into a bath formed by the solution of some antiseptic in powder, which the late Mr. Frank Buckland had procured for me. The bath totally destroyed the beauty of colours of the fish, and turned them into a dirty brown, but I ate one of those fish on the Saturday after in perfectly good condition and flavour, and I could have eaten the other in the same state, so far as the flesh went, on the Saturday after that again, but the flies had got at the gills, and the idea was distasteful. I wrote for some more of the disinfectant, and the reply that I got was that the company was in liquidation, and that I could have the patent for £1,000; so I thought no more of the matter and have forgotten the name of the disinfectant. I only mention the matter to show of what service antiseptics may be.

The drift fishery of which I have been speaking is the principal mackerel fishery now, and supplies us with practically the whole of this fish. The few thousand mackerel taken at present each year in seines are wholly absorbed in strictly local markets. The mackerel takes bait, but, generally speaking, shyly. Every five or six years they turn up in large shoals, which are intensely localised, in the autumn and for about two hours a day, in the evening, for a week or ten days, take surface bait greedily. I, myself, once cruising backwards and forwards over a little patch of ground (where a shoal of this sort had located itself), for about two hours between five and eight on each evening, for four days in August month, took, on a whiffing or light hand-line and on a hook baited with a strip cut from an old white kid glove, over three hundred fish. I have known the mackerel to be in shoals in December, but this is rare. When they do occur in that month they are small but in excellent condition as food.

Before I pass away from the mackerel, on which I have detained you a great deal too long, I wish to tell you of another discovery of mine, which no doubt equally affects all fish; but as my observation of it was made on mackerel, I confine my narrative to that fish. Its habit of shoaling in the daytime taught me the curious fact that the shoal leaves behind it a distinct scent in the water, and that there are other inhabitants of the sea who quite understand what that scent means, and utilize it.

A shoal of fish in the water looks, at a distance, like the shadow of a cloud moving steadily on. As the shade nears you, you can see the fish "playing," jumping out of the water just as small trout do, only in a large shoal you will see thousands of fish out of the water at the same time. Each sort of fish gives a colour to the water which is peculiar to it, so that an experienced fisherman knows at sight whether the shadow of the cloud, which he knows to be a shoal of fish, covers mackerel, or pilchard, or herring, or sprat. I was once standing on the beach with an old fisherman when we saw a straggling shoal of fish about half-a-mile long, swimming very slowly, which we could not make out. Their colour was new to him. So we took a boat and went out to them, and found they were a shoal of huge jelly fish, great transparent things shaped like an open umbrella and about its size, having around the edge of the umbrella a beautiful purple fringe which causes you to recollect it if you incautiously touch it. On the occasion to which I refer I was standing on a headland in a place called Prussia Cove, in Mount's Bay, when I saw a shoal, which I knew at once to be of mackerel, come out of a sandy bay there and go due west.

Shortly after I saw a shoal of porpoises (a cetacean which loves the mackerel in an epicurean sense) come lumbering up from the south into the sand. When they came across the trail of the mackerel these latter were a good mile off on their way. The porpoises had no sooner got into their back water than they wheeled into their course and set off in full chase. In about three minutes they were in the midst of the mackerel, playing havoc, whilst the unfortunate mackerel were driving forward in one solid line of terror, making the water foam before them as they fled.

Of the Pilchard I have a different tale to tell. It is a little fish of the "herring" family, generally about ten inches long, and rarely so much as half a pound in weight. It is very local in its habits, rarely occurring in numbers of any importance east of the Start Point, in Devonshire, on the South coast, and Trevose Head, in Cornwall, on the north. It is taken yearly as far east as the estuary of the Exe, and has been taken, and occasionally in large numbers, off Seaton, in Devonshire, at the mouth of the river Axe. Some years since a small shoal was taken off Folkestone.*

It occurs in very large numbers off the south-west coast of Ireland, but there is no native fishery for it there, and as its season on that coast coincides with its season on ours, our people are too busy at home to look after it. It occurs, of course, off the French coasts as the sardine. And the Spaniards have a mode of curing it which altogether beats our English method, as may be seen by a comparison of our

---

* There is also some record of the capture of a shoal at Harwich, and a fish supposed to be the pilchard occurs in Scotland under the name of the garvie herring, but practically its home in England is in Cornwall and mainly in West Cornwall.

cured pilchards in this exhibition with those in the Spanish division.*

Unlike the mackerel, the pilchard is not sought for in its fresh state out of Cornwall and West Devon. Our fishermen have tried many markets with it, but without success. And this is the more remarkable seeing that the fish is cheap, nutritious, and of exceedingly good flavour. When tourists first found out West Cornwall, they very soon found out pilchards, and more, they turned a little bit of "chaff" against us west countrymen into a reality, at their own expense. It used to be said of us that we ate "cream with our pilchards," which of course we never did. But when the tourist came down, he took it for granted that he could eat clotted cream with everything, and he insisted on having "cream with his pilchard," and he is said to have got it, and to have found it so good a mixture that now no large hotel gives broiled pilchard for breakfast without it.†

But we have other ways of cooking them besides broiling. We fry them and eat them with a sauce made of finely chopped onions, salt, cold water, and nothing else; it is a very nasty sauce. And we eat them without any knives or forks, with our fingers. I do not say that *all* of us do this, but I have seen it done, and less than one hundred years ago the practice was universal amongst the bulk of our people.

I hope to cure this want of a fresh pilchard market soon

---

* There are two open barrels of the fish exhibited one at each end of the westernmost case in the Spanish Court. One is labelled "pressed sardines," and the other "salted sardines," but they are both of them pilchards, more cleanly cured than is our wont.

† I can speak to the excellency of clotted cream as a sauce with broiled pilchard from personal experience.

in this building. I hope to induce some of our fisher people to send a supply to the fish-market here so soon as the season opens, which it will in a few weeks, and I think that with the great advantages offered here, we may succeed where others, under less favourable circumstances, have failed. Spain is running us so close in the business of supplying salted pilchards for the markets of the Roman Catholic countries, that we could easily find thirty to forty millions of fish for the supply of a fresh fish market without feeling the loss of them. This apparently enormous number would be a mere flea-bite out of our catch for a season. It would be a day's, or at most two day's successful fishing for the seines of St. Ives alone. And this brings me to the support of Professor Huxley in his remark, that in the waters frequented by the pilchard the sea, taken acre for acre, is of greater pecuniary value than the land. A seine when "shot" around a shoal of pilchards may enclose an acre of superficial water, certainly not more than two. It is on record that the seines in St. Ives Bay did on one occasion, in one day, capture 10,000 hogsheads, or over 30 millions of pilchards, worth, over the boat's side, £2 per hogshead. I do not know the number of seines employed, but they could not possibly have exceeded 20; but, supposing they were 20, then 20 acres, or at the highest figure 40 acres of sea yielded £20,000 as its produce for one day, and each season consists of many days, and the fisherman pays no rent.*

* The greatest recorded catch by one seine at one shot was made at St. Ives in 1868. There 5,600 hogsheads, or over 16 millions of pilchards, were saved out of one seine. This catch was worth between £11,000 and £12,000. Remarks of precisely the same character, but differing in detail, apply to our trawling grounds, but as pilchards are never taken by the trawler, I only allude to this fact.

Since I wrote the above about opening up a cheap market for small dainty fish like the pilchard, the question, as one intended to benefit the poorer classes, has been placed before me in what is to me an entirely new light. And it is this: Supposing you can supply pilchards in the height of their season at one penny each over the fish-stall (and the remark applies to all other fish which could be sold cheap), what is the poor man to do with it? In summer he must go to the expense of a fire to cook it. At any time he must provide fat in which to fry it, most of which will be wasted, and after all, the chances are that his wife does not know how to cook it, and will spoil the dish in the doing of it. And for this, my practical informant says, there is but one remedy. If you want to introduce cheap fish for the use of the artisan you must in some way or other start shops or whatever places you like where he can get it cooked. Most of these difficulties apply also to the dressing of fish by boiling, but my informant adds to these another, that the prejudice against boiled fish is at present so deep-seated as to be practically ineradicable.

You will find in this building, pilchards cured by all the methods in use, salted in barrels for the foreign market, dressed in oil, as sardines, or in salt sauce, as anchovies, or marinated, which is, I believe, an invention of our own; and in every form you will find them good.

The method in which the pilchards are cured for the Italian market expresses from them when "in bulk" (i.e., under the pressure in large masses necessary for salting them) large quantities of blood, which run from the curing-house down the streets in gutters to the sea. We are a toast-drinking people, and this peculiarity in the curing process gave rise to a toast which used to be given as equivalent to prosperity to the pilchard fishery. It was:—

"Long life to the Pope, and may our streets run with blood."

The fish itself resembles a small silvery herring having large scales. The people who catch it are much the same as those who fish for mackerel, but the fishery has a separate capital invested in it, the boats and nets used being peculiar to it.

It is captured in much the same way as the mackerel is. In the night in drift nets; in the day time in seines. Originally pilchard seining and mackerel seining were conducted in much the same way, but the decline of mackerel seining has now-a-days caused them to differ.

The lookout of a mackerel seine is mostly kept on board the boat itself, and the seine net is hauled bodily on board with the fish in it, but in pilchard seining the lookout is kept from some hill where the huer—or man stationed to watch for the shoals of fish—can be seen from the boat, standing clear out against the sky. He thus gets a much wider outlook than can be had from the boat. He holds in each hand a bush, and when he sights a shoal of fish he informs the boat of its whereabouts by preconcerted signals made with these bushes. The seine boat moves in the direction indicated, and if it reaches the shoal in time it shoots its net. You must consider of this net when shot, as a round room in the water without a floor or ceiling, and if the shot is successful it contains the pilchards. At the next low water time a net, called a tuck net, and which I will liken to a perforated pocket handkerchief, is let down from large boats stationed at one side of the room of water, the tuck-net being inside the seine, and it is drawn up by means of ropes hauled in on board large boats stationed for the purpose at the other side so as to scoop up the fish in the seine. As the ropes come home the boats close in upon the net, and then a very exciting, and on moonlight nights a very beautiful scene sets in. Millions of silvery little fish are sputtering and clattering on the surface of the water in the tuck-net. Half a dozen men are in the midst of them up to their knees in fish, handing them into the boats in baskets, and working for dear life. Everybody is giving orders at the top of his voice about everything, and nobody is obeying anybody, and so the work goes on until the coming tide stops them, and causes them to run the risk of the escape of the fish before the next low water. Most of the fish thus caught are salted for export, but many find their way through the locality of their capture in the cowels or baskets exhibited on our Cornwall stall, and which are worn in the picturesque way shown in the lithograph also exhibited there. A strong woman can carry 1 cwt. of fish in the way shown, and for miles.

But the waving of a huer's bushes has a very curious effect on any fishing village which happens to get sight, or news of it. To the stranger it would appear that the whole population of the place had suddenly gone lunatic. Every available man, woman and child turns out and rushes violently down the steep cliff to the sea shouting "heva! heva!" Whence the word is derived, we do not know; but it is the signal that shoaling fish are in sight, and that the population must turn out to be ready to receive them, for all this fish-work requires to be done with the utmost dispatch.

A very curious thing, and entirely inexplicable, about these shoaling pilchards, is that at uncertain periods they shift their course for years together. For instance, fifty years ago, St. Ives on our North coast had almost a monopoly of the shoaling pilchard; now she divides with

Newquay. Thirty-five years ago the principal South coast scining fishery was in Mount's Bay, now it is at Mevagissey, and it is no question of new seine fisheries having been established. It is due solely and entirely to a change of habitat on the part of the fish. We have many things yet to learn about the pilchard.

One thing I have learned since I began to write this paper, is that during the mackerel season (February to June) and before our pilchard season commences, numerous shoals of very large pilchards are met with by our mackerel drivers in the deep sea, eight leagues and over, south and west of the Scilly Islands. These large pilchards are mostly females full of roe, ready to be shed, and unlike most fish in that condition are so dry and tasteless as to be utterly useless as food. A test of their size is that they are taken in the meshes of the mackerel nets.

Like the mackerel the pilchard is not a true migrant, but comes in from the deep sea, shoaling by day and scattering by night, and remains on for its season. Unlike the mackerel it never takes a bait,* and is but very rarely seen in our seas except in its season; but again, like the mackerel, it is too thorough a nomad to stand the confinement of an aquarium. And those of you who wish to see either of them alive must seek for them in their native haunts.

* Whilst this paper was in the press information reached me that a pilchard had been captured, hooked in the mouth, on a white-feather whiffing-fly; but as two other pilchards were at the same time captured, hooked in the side, it is probable that they were all accidently hooked out of a shoal through which the whiffing-line was passing. The fish may have been playing with the fly rather than attempting to feed on it.

DISCUSSION.

Professor BROWN GOODE said he had heard some complaint that there were too many scientific men on the platform in these conferences, and too few practical men, but every one would agree that Mr. Cornish had shown that he had a thorough practical acquaintance with the subject, whilst he had used a thoroughly scientific method in his deductions. He had listened with great pleasure to the Paper, having been for some years paying special attention to the mackerel fishery in the United States. That fishery was one of the most important in the American waters. The produce in the year 1880 was about 132,000,000 pounds. It employed about 470 of their finest sea-going schooners, of from 60 to 100 tons burden each, and with an aggregate capacity of about 23,000 tons, with crews of 14 to 20 men, and nets worth 450,000 dollars or more. Within the last few years, since the introduction of the purse net to which Mr. Cornish had referred, it was not uncommon for one of those vessels to catch fish to the value of £5000 or even £7500 a year. The history of the mackerel fishery was very interesting. As long ago as the year 1600, within forty years of the settlement in New England, there were records of the colonists seining the mackerel off Cape Cod by moonlight; and it was somewhat remarkable, that on this fishery was founded the system of public schools in the United States, for within ten or twenty years of that time the first public school was founded on a tax upon the fishery. At that time, when perhaps not one hundred barrels a year were taken, they found the inhabitants petitioning to prevent the destruction of the mackerel by this method of fishing, and that appeal had been repeated at various times in the history of the fisheries, even down to the present time. In the American Court of the Exhibition could be seen a diagram showing the progress of the mackerel fishery, and the very great fluctuations which took place not only with reference to the quantity of fish caught, but the number of vessels employed. It would be noticed that in 1882 the catch was very much greater than in any previous year, so that the fears as to the destruction of the fish did not seem to be well founded. Two methods of fishing were afterwards introduced; first, the gill net or drag net, like that used in Cornwall, and which is still used to a limited extent at the present time. Another method introduced about the same time, and kept up for a considerable period, was what they called trailing, or dragging a bait after a vessel under sail. That was carried on until the beginning of this century, and it was not uncommon to see a vessel with four or five poles sticking out from it, to which the bait was attached. That was given up, however, fifty years ago. At the beginning of this century another form of apparatus came into use, which was exceedingly effective for a time, and it was during the prevalence of this method that the great fisheries in the United States and the Canadian waters sprung up which had led to so many treaties from 1865 to 1870. There were from 500 to 700, or even in some years 1000 American vessels in the Gulf of St. Lawrence fishing for mackerel, and this was called the mackerel hook fishery. It was conducted in this way: the fishermen took on board a hundred or more barrels of a very oily, fat fish called the menhaden, something like the pilchard. They ground it up fine and threw it out in great quantities. The mackerel would follow this for a long distance, and come up round the vessel like a flock of chickens coming to be fed. Then the fishermen had short lines with hooks on the ends, with which they caught the mackerel and threw them over on to the deck, and with a crew of 10 to 14 men the catch would sometimes amount to 20,000 in a day. That mode of fishing was carried on for a long time, but the purse seine gradually came into use and displaced it. It was first used in 1814, but did not come into general use until 1860, and there were now probably 500 of them at work. The mackerel fishery had now been transferred from the Gulf of St. Lawrence to off the shore waters along the coast, and at the present time they followed them down to Cape Hatteras. The mackerel on the other side of the Atlantic had definite migrations, coming north in the spring of the year, when the fishermen followed them until August, when they were in the Gulf of Maine, then they followed them back in the fall. The mackerel increased in size as they got on better feeding-ground. They disappeared for a month or so in June, when they went to the bottom and spawned. He could assure Mr. Cornish that there was not the slightest practical difficulty in working the purse seine. They were from 70 to 150 feet in depth, and 1,000 to 1,300 in length, and were worked by a special boat something like a whale boat, and it was quite easy for a vessel to catch as many fish as could be cured in three or four days. At first they used to give the surplus away or let them go, but now they had invented a kind of storage net, which they hung out over the side of the vessel, and kept the fish alive in it, taking out at intervals as many as they could cure before they spoiled.

Mr. KENNETH CORNISH asked if Mr. Cornish was in favour of legislation for the preservation of mackerel? Referring to what had been said in regard to the pursuit of herrings and mackerel by porpoises, he might say that he witnessed a very remarkable sight at Teignmouth in the year 1860. In walking along the sea wall they saw a great commotion in the sea, a mile out, and watching it, they soon found a shoal of salmon running in, pursued by a shoal of large grampuses, who drove the unfortunate salmon right against the wall. They seized the salmon in their jaws, threw them up, and caught them like a terrier would a rat, and when the salmon turned and went out to sea again, they pursued them. He should like to know if Mr. Cornish thought it possible to catch these cetacea, seals and other animals that preyed on salmon. herrings, and mackerel, by the use of spinning bait on a large scale? It seemed to him we were thinning down the fish, but not thinning down their natural enemies. It would not be at all difficult to make baits which would exactly represent a salmon, mackerel, or herring, with hooks concealed internally; and they might even be impregnated with the natural flavour of the fish.

Mr. CORNISH, in reply, said, as far as his experience went, he did not think legislation was required with respect to a close time for mackerel or pilchards; they took a close time for themselves and got away where they could not be caught. Further legislation was very desirable for the purpose of regulating the fishing of our own boats in British waters; and even if what legislation there was were better enforced, it would be of great importance. With regard to catching porpoises, he should not like to tackle one weighing more than 2 cwt. in a small boat.

Mr. SHAW, M.P., in moving a vote of thanks to Mr.

Cornish, said he was much interested in the mackerel fishing of the south coast of Ireland; but he had learnt a great deal he did not know before. Up to the present he always thought that if a mackerel could speak it would talk Irish, but he was now pretty well convinced that it would also speak in Cornish; and perhaps if it could speak in either language it could give a different account of its sufferings to that which had been given in the Paper. One thing, however, might mitigate one's sympathies in this respect, for mackerel had not the slightest regard for other fish which suited its taste. In the neighbourhood of Cork there was a fleet of five hundred boats engaged in the mackerel fishery. He was sorry to say there were not as many native Irish engaged in it as he could desire, because round that part of the coast the inhabitants were a poor class of men, with very little enterprise, and very few of them were men of business or capital. In another district, too, mackerel fishing had been established, and seemed likely to succeed; and he should be very much wanting in his duty if he did not refer to the great help given there by Lady Burdett Coutts, but for whose assistance the thing could not have existed. It was very satisfactory to know that the people of the coast—a simple primitive people—had availed themselves of the assistance offered them, and there were some of the best boats engaged in the fishery now going from the Harbour of Baltimore on the south coast of Ireland. The great object of catching fish was to bring it as quickly and cheaply as possible to the table, and he did not think there was a better fishing ground in the world than that round the south coast of Cork; but hitherto facilities of transport had been rather deficient. Now, however, they were in a much better position in this respect, as there were rails now touching the fishing grounds at Kinsale, Skibbereen, Baltimore, and Bantry, and in the Bay of Bantry a steamer had been put on, so that every evening the fish caught in any of those places could be shipped, and next day it would be delivered in the cities and towns of England. The great thing to be desired was to have as few people as possible between the consumer and the fishermen, otherwise the profit was scattered about by the number of hands through which the fish passed. If there were any gentlemen present engaged in the fish business, he would recommend them to send their agents over there, who would day by day collect the fish and send it forward. He knew, from practical experience, that fishermen got very little as the result of their industry; this did not apply so much to the mackerel fishery, because it was mostly conducted by men of skill and experience who could take care of themselves.

Mr. C. E. FRYER had great pleasure in seconding the vote of thanks. The Chairman had referred to the beautiful scene presented at night when the boats were leaving the harbour, but it appeared to him the enjoyment was much enhanced when you happened to be on board one of the vessels going to the fishing grounds. Having had the pleasure himself, he could recommend any one who visited Cornwall to endeavour to get a night's fishing on board one of those boats; for no more beautiful scene could be imagined than was presented on a fine evening on board a boat off the Land's End. The energy of the Cornish fishermen had been referred to, but, like many others engaged in the same vocation, they were remarkably conservative in their habits, and it was very difficult to induce them to adopt improved methods of fishing. He had had the great satisfaction of introducing into this country the system of preserving pilchards in oil, in the manner in which sardines were preserved in France. There could be no question that the sardine was exactly the same fish as the pilchard, and those who had not tasted them he would recommend to buy in future not the French sardines but the Cornish. He had no interest personally in giving this advice, beyond the desire of seeing an industry which he had established prospering to the extent which it deserved. As an instance of the difficulty of inducing the fishermen to take a "new departure" in fishery matters, he related that on one occasion, when off Penzance, he endeavoured to get the fishermen to put aside the smaller fish, for the purpose of preserving them as sardines, as it was found that the smaller ones were preferred for the purpose, but he had the greatest difficulty in the world to induce the fishermen to adopt that simple precaution. Every fish had to be taken out of the net, and it would have been perfectly easy for the men to put the small ones on one side and the large ones on the other, but their conservative tendencies prevailed, and they would not take the trouble to do so. There was a saying that the Cornish people could make anything into a pie ; and it was said that if a certain gentleman, who should be nameless, were to go there, he would be put into a pie ; and just as they were determined to put everything into a pie, so were they loth to adopt new methods of preserving fish for the market. If proper means were adopted there was no reason why enormous quantities of pilchards, preserved in salt as well as in tins, should not be sent to London and other English markets, though of course there were difficulties of transport to be overcome. Mr. Cornish had referred to the remarkable occasional disappearance of the pilchard from the coast of Cornwall, and it occurred to him that possibly the china clay works in Cornwall might have some influence on the movements of those fish. Enormous quantities of milk-white water were poured into the sea down many small streams in the county, and that might have some effect, though he did not suppose it was the chief cause of the disappearance, because the same sudden disappearance had been noticed in France. He recently came across a letter received in 1879 from a friend in France, who spoke of the sudden appearance there of the sardines in great abundance, though for more than twenty years there had been a great scarcity. The abundance which had generally prevailed since had shown large occasional fluctuations. He trusted that many other gentlemen in Cornwall would follow Mr. Cornish's example, and make a study of the movements of this and other fish with a view to the practical encouragement of those very important industries.

The resolution having been carried unanimously

Mr. CORNISH said he did not think the china clay had much to do with the disappearance of fish, because it had been noticed that they still remained in localities where that water and also mineral water ran into the sea. They would require to watch them still more closely for some time to find out the reason for those movements.

The MARQUIS OF EXETER then proposed a vote of thanks to the Chairman for presiding. Mr. Cornish had alluded to three kinds of mackerel, one of which, the green, was unwholesome; and he was glad to hear the explanation, because not long ago his crew, who were Irish, came one morning and said they were all very bad from eating mackerel that had been in the moonlight. He concluded that it was this green mackerel. He had oftentimes enjoyed the pleasure of fishing off the Cornish coast, and had always met with the greatest kindness from fishermen and others; and he could recommend any one who wanted a good fishing ground where they could catch all manner of fish, to go, when the wind was not to the south or west, and lie off Penzance. They might catch there every kind of fish, from the mackerel down to the beautiful jelly-fish which Mr. Cornish had alluded to, which he had often watched on a calm day struggling to make head against the tide, but eventually drifting with it; and perhaps the Chairman would recollect that they had it on the authority of a noble duke, that certain friends of his, who were as brilliant in talents as these jelly-fish were in colour, were also in the habit of drifting with the tide.

Mr. HORNBLOWER seconded the motion, which was carried unanimously.

The CHAIRMAN, in response, said it had given him much pleasure to be present at a discussion of so practical a character. There were many points on which he should have liked to touch had the time not been so far advanced, but he would only say, in correction of what Mr. Fryer had said, that the Cornish proverb was that the devil would not come into Cornwall because he was afraid of being put into a pie.

International Fisheries Exhibition,
LONDON, 1883.

THE

HERRING FISHERIES.

BY

H. J. GREEN.

[*PRIZE ESSAY.*]

LONDON:
WILLIAM CLOWES AND SONS, Limited,
13 CHARING CROSS, S.W.
1884.

LONDON:
PRINTED BY WILLIAM CLOWES AND SONS, LIMITED,
STAMFORD STREET AND CHARING CROSS.

THE HERRING FISHERIES.

THE increasing interest shown year after year in all matters connected with our fisheries is a sign of the times that can neither be overlooked nor under-valued. It is practically a recantation of the doctrine that the subject was one merely concerning professors and students of natural history, and an acknowledgment that, considered with reference to British industry and commerce, it is a matter of paramount importance. One of the most interesting divisions of the fisheries is the herring fishery. It is interesting, not only on account of the large number of persons which it employs, and its influence on the country financially, but on account of the natural history of the herring, of the theories which have been advanced and overthrown respecting its migration, and of the veil of mystery which for a long time hid the secret of its reproduction from human understanding. It is obvious that whatever tends to elucidate and clear up disputed points in its natural history must react in a beneficial manner commercially. The record of the last few years has been far from being a blank page in this respect; but perhaps, for the sake of completeness, it will be well to state a few of the earlier facts ascertained of the natural history of the herring.

Let us consider first, then, the senses of the herring. They have been the subject of much difference of opinion, as indeed they have been concerning all fish. Yet the organs, though of course very minute, are so distinctly formed that we cannot avoid coming to the conclusion that they were meant to be used. The tongue, for instance, is very small, but there is no doubt about a tongue being there; and what is a tongue there for if not to be used? It is true that the senses of taste and smell of some of our fish are not always very correct, especially of those who prefer the neighbourhood of sewers and drains; but they are the exceptions which prove the rule. Then, as regards hearing, the balance of evidence seems to be in favour of their being endowed with that sense. We need not question whether they are able to see or not.

One of the most important points to be ascertained with certainty is—what constitutes the chief food of the herring? There has been much diversity of opinion on this matter; but it appears to be pretty clear that the herring does not feed upon one kind of food. The preference seems to be for small crustacea, although worms and the eggs of fishes have been found in their stomachs, and even young herrings. It will thus be seen that the cultivation of crustacea has a very important bearing on the prosperity of the fisheries; for we cannot hope to bring the latter to a high degree of efficiency if the food supply is not promoted in a corresponding degree. It is a noticeable fact that herrings caught in lochs and bays are superior in quality to those caught on the open sea-coast. What is the reason of this? Is it that the food is more abundant or more suitable? It is a point worth investigation.

The next important point to be solved is the settlement of the period of the year when they spawn. On the satisfactory solution of this problem the very existence of the fishery greatly depends. If we do not know when to look for the fish, we cannot catch them; therefore anything that adds to our knowledge on this point is a very material assistance. A great many of our eminent men are of opinion that the herring spawns twice a year. We know, however, for certain that herrings appear at different times at different places; and the investigations of the last few years have led us to believe that the object of their appearance off the coasts is for the operation of spawning. For instance, at Wick they appear between July and September; at Eyemouth between June and September; at Arran between July and November; and at Thurso as early as May. In the Moray Firth the time is from June to September, but in the Firth of Forth it is from November to March. [It may be noted incidentally that the Scotch fishery of last year was very successful.] In England we find the herrings at Yarmouth between June and November, off Cornwall in August and September, off Kent in October and November, and off Yorkshire between July and September. In Ireland they are fished at Galway in September; off Kerry between January and March; and in the Irish Channel between June and November. Taken as a general rule, we may say that the winter herring generally spawns in February and March, and the summer—or autumn?—herring in September and October.

It is an easy transition from the subject of their spawning time to the subject of their migration, or supposed migration. There was a time—and we should not have to go back very far—when the theory of their migration from the Arctic regions was most stoutly maintained. We know better now. The interesting story was to the effect that the normal abode of the herrings was in the Arctic seas, and that they made periodical visits to the south (led by an advanced guard of one or two fishes!) for the purpose of spawning. Little was wanting to complete this dramatic story. We knew that the herrings usually lived in the North; we knew that they sometimes came to the south; we knew that they divided off the north of Scotland, one corps going to the right and the other to the left,—all that was wanted were the herrings themselves. There is not, however, a shadow of a doubt about our previous belief being a huge mistake. The herring inhabits the deep water round our coasts all the year round, and comes periodically towards the shore to propagate its kind. The chief argument that has been set up in favour of this statement is, that year after year, and at the same time of the year, we always find the same kind of herring in the same place. It is therefore a very reasonable assumption that they are in the neighbourhood all the year round. Besides, herrings caught in the extreme north of Scotland are inferior and lean compared to those caught at the same time farther south, which should not be the condition of herrings that are just about to spawn. Whether there are any who still believe in the migration of the herrings from the Polar regions—and we would remind them that they must also believe in the advanced guard story, too—matters little; it is enough that a very large number of persons have long since abandoned it and accepted the other theory.

The next point on which we would willingly have more information is—what period elapses between the time of depositing the spawn and the appearance of the young fish?

This is a matter very difficult to ascertain, chiefly from the difficulty experienced in observing the operation; but we may take it that the eggs are converted into fish in a fortnight or three weeks. In about nine weeks' time the fish are 3 or 4 inches long, and are full-grown herrings in about a year and a half. Any information on the latter point would also be extremely useful. It would dissipate some doubts as to when the operation of spawning is performed for the first time by the young herring.

After all, it must be confessed with regret that our knowledge of the natural history of the herring is exceedingly limited. It has been thought that we may learn a good deal from those whose vocation it is to catch them. That, however, is very far from being the case. The ignorance among the fishermen of the habits of the herring is certainly not very flattering to our insular pride. That it betrays a want of observation on their part, or incapacity to connect their observations with their occupation, cannot be denied. Perhaps the remedy might be found in erecting schools for fisher-boys, where the young generation might learn something of elementary Natural History that might act as an incentive to further observation of animated nature. The aim of all knowledge should be to apply it to the affairs of our every-day life.

A study of the fisheries of other countries is always interesting, and often instructive. We may in this way often learn methods of capture and curing, that may be profitably followed by ourselves; and we may also gather fresh facts concerning the natural history of the fish. It is but fitting to commence with a reference to the Dutch fisheries. We cannot help feeling a respect and admiration for a people who once possessed the finest fisheries in the world. We recall with envy the picture of their former superiority, a superiority which has long since passed away. The naturalists tell us that their superiority was owing to their fishing on our coasts in our absence on other matters. Whether that was the case or not we cannot say; but even supposing that it was, it looks as if the Dutch still deserved the palm for superior strategy. While, however, we willingly accord whatever praise is due to the Dutch, we are far from endorsing the extravagant eulogy that many have thought fit to bestow on them. The Dutch fishermen of old acquired, and for a long time maintained, their proud position by their method of curing herrings. It is somewhat strange that, great as England was in many respects at the meridian of Dutch prosperity, she should have been so far behind in this matter. Probably those great events of the time of Elizabeth were themselves the cause. The people were too much occupied by foreign affairs to attend to humbler matters at home. The Dutch fishermen kept their secrets pretty much to themselves; but it will probably be found that they owed much of their success to their curing the herrings immediately they were hauled up from the sea.

The French fishery is chiefly remarkable for the cure of sprats (about which we shall have something more to say presently) in oil.

The Norwegian fishery is noted for various methods of smoking the young herring.

A very interesting mode of fishing under difficulties is practised in Russia. Owing to the severe climate of that country, and to the consequent freezing of the water, the fishing industry is much curtailed; but the fishermen manage to secure a good many fish by making lines of holes in the ice, and inserting their nets in them.

It may not be inappropriate to say something here about the whitebait, the sprat, and the pilchard. As regards the whitebait, the question that chiefly interests us is whether it is the young of the herring or not. For a long time naturalists held that it was not; and there is a good deal that might seem to support that view. The head of the whitebait was thought to differ slightly from the head of the herring; the comparative length of the head to the rest of the body was supposed to differ, and the body itself was flatter than the herring, and lighter in colour. But there is an argument that completely over-rules and destroys these minor objections, viz. that the whitebait is never found with milt or roe. This, to our mind, taken in conjunction with the fact that large quantities are sometimes caught with herrings, demonstrates very clearly that the whitebait is the offspring of the herring. The length of the whitebait is between two and four inches, and, very rarely, five inches. It is very plentiful in the Firth of Forth, and in the Thames, and is sometimes found in the Clyde and other rivers.

The sprat is also an interesting fish. It has been accused of following the example of the whitebait; but, although it is remarkable that sprats are taken in large numbers with herrings, we will not, on our present knowledge, go so far as to say that they are the offspring of the herring. There is some relationship between the two. However, the fact of sprats having milt and roe at the proper spawning-time seems to show that they are not the young of the herring. The sprat fishery commences in November, and lasts till February or March. The principal coasts on which it is prosecuted are Norfolk, Suffolk, Essex, and Kent.

The pilchard resembles the herring in some respects, although there are important differences both in the formation and in the habits of the two. For instance, the scales of the pilchard are larger than those of the herring. Again, the pilchard will rest in a horizontal position if suspended by the dorsal fin; while the herring dips towards the head.

Further, the pilchard has an exceedingly limited distribution, while the herring has a very wide distribution. The pilchard fishery generally commences about July, and continues to December. Like the herring, the pilchard is a migratory fish, lives in the deep water, and approaches the shores to spawn. The coasts that it most frequents are those of Devon and Cornwall; in fact, we may say that the fishery is confined to those counties, and the fish appear in great numbers.

There is yet one other digression that we would make. Scotland has the honour of being the home of two very puzzling fish, namely, the powan of Loch Lomond and the vendace of Lochmaben. Careful observation has "almost persuaded" naturalists to believe these fish to be descendants of herrings; and the reason they assign for the existence of the fish in fresh water is that the monks of old, who, it is to be presumed, lived largely on fish, brought them there. The habits of the fish certainly very much resemble those of herrings.

We will now consider the question of the herring brand. A very slight examination of the subject will suffice to show that the system is opposed to the principles that should regulate trade. It is true the brand is not compulsory, which, while robbing it of many objections, really amounts to very little, because every large curer is bound to use it for the simple reason that everybody else does. The brand, however, is very useful to small curers, because it gives them a chance of competing with the large curers. But it is a distinct form of State interference—an interference in the sale of an article of extensive consumption. What are the reasons that can sanction such an arrangement? Why are not our potatoes, and cabbages, and boots, and chairs and tables branded? The chief reason that can be urged in favour of the continuance of the brand is that it is convenient for foreign trade. The brand has been in existence for so many years that the buyers in foreign countries have learnt to regard it as a guarantee that they are not being cheated. Barrels bearing the Crown brand are never waiting for a buyer, and they are passed on from hand to hand with nearly as much convenience as paper money. We cannot deny, either, that the system greatly assists the people in their purchases by the rejection of inferior fish. It is best as a rule to choose for ourselves, but there are certain occasions when the judgment of a skilled officer is preferable to our own. In the next place, those whom the question most nearly affects are in favour of the continuance of the brand. If those who are most nearly concerned are content to pay the small fee for the brand to the Scotch Fishery Board, it certainly seems unwise and unnecessary to disturb a system that has worked so well.

We have here, then, a remarkable instance of a system undoubtedly wrong in principle working well in practice. It would seem that our objects have been accomplished by means which are open to question. Nevertheless, although, in the circumstances, we would wish to see this particular system maintained, we strongly disapprove of it for other articles. No fresh system should be *started* on these principles. It may be urged that a fresh system would become as successful as this has become. We think not. This system was instituted when the fishery was comparatively undeveloped, and therefore, having grown with it, the system has become, as it were, a part of the fishery. But to start a similar system now, in connection with an article of extensive use, would be a decided mistake. We may depend upon it that the less we have of Government interference the better it will be for us. There are, of course, a few matters, such as the regulation of cab-fares, that are, for simple convenience, best done by the Government. But it is a dangerous principle. It has led to tyranny in the past, and it may lead to tyranny in the future. The times have passed—we trust for ever—when justice was openly bought and sold, and when monopolies were bartered for political objects. We cannot forget those days, never to be recalled without a feeling of shame, when one class was raised by the degradation of another. It is a dark page in our history; but it is, nevertheless, one that must be guarded against for the future. If ever the time should come when Englishmen will submit to all trade being arrested by imposts and fetters, we confess that we should have little hope for the future of England. Are we to be treated as children—as persons who are incapable of judging for themselves? No; the noblest aim of man should be to think and act for himself, to exercise the intellect with which God has endowed him above every other creature, and to contribute as far as in him lays to the sum of human happiness.

LONDON: PRINTED BY WILLIAM CLOWES AND SONS, LIMITED,
STAMFORD STREET AND CHARING CROSS.

International Fisheries Exhibition,
LONDON, 1883.

THE

HERRING FISHERIES.

BY

R. J. MUNRO.

[*PRIZE ESSAY.*]

LONDON:
WILLIAM CLOWES AND SONS, Limited,
13 CHARING CROSS, S.W.
1884.

LONDON:
PRINTED BY WILLIAM CLOWES AND SONS, LIMITED,
STAMFORD STREET AND CHARING CROSS.

CONTENTS.

	PAGE
Around the Coast and order of the British Herring Fishery—Close time wanted	3
Curing herring by machinery	5
The West Coast—The Best Coast	6
Great Yarmouth—Historical notices, and mode of curing herrings	7
Irish and West Coast of England Herring Fishery	10
Iceland—Prospects at Shetland—Loss of life, &c.	12
Herring Fisheries of Norway, Sweden, and Denmark—Modes of curing	13
Holland and Dutch cured herrings	15
Nova Scotia, Newfoundland, and North American coasts—Specimens of the Clupeidæ family, &c., &c.	17
Largest takes of herring yet recorded for the West Coast in February and March 1883	19
Harbour accommodation—Coasting steamers—Uncertainty of the season—Causes assigned	20
Winter Fishery on the East Coast of Scotland and statistics for the year (1883)—Sprat Fishery, &c.	24
Table showing total catches over the entire East Coast of Scotland for past twenty-six years	25
Quantities branded for past twenty-six years	25
Exports from Wick to Continental, Irish, English and Scotch ports for past ten years	26
Total catch at each station from Northumberland to Shetland during past ten years	27
Food of the herring—Spawning, Temperature, &c.	29
Allegations against trawlers—Remedies—Other grievances	30
Fish Culture *versus* Trawling — Herring spawn — The old Mesh — Statistics for England desirable, and total quantities landed at Great Yarmouth	34
Scotland, the leading Herring Fishery of the World—Bounty system illustrated	35
Leading centres in Scotland, and largest exports those of 1882—Comparative table for Fraserburgh	36
Curing process—The "Brand Question," and merits of cure—Stettin Report, &c.	37
Distinguishing features and structure of the herring — Habitat — Frequency of spawning process	39
Commissioners' Report—New method of fishing with old nets, &c.	41

THE HERRING FISHERIES.

PART I.

THE herring fisheries form one of the greatest commercial sea enterprises at home or abroad as a ready source of wealth. Royalty has aided its development, for it is branded from olden time by the legislative care of kings and governments. In England this fishery was pursued at a very early period. Yarmouth was taxed to the amount of ten thousand herrings for his Majesty King Henry I. Edward III. encouraged and fostered this industry with money and wise legislation. In Scotland, also, it has had the patronage of royalty, especially from their Majesties James V. and VI. And to this present time Parliament has passed many Acts and inquiries affecting our herring fisheries.

The British herring fishery is inaugurated at the Hebrides in the month of May, and closes with the autumn and winter fishery at Yarmouth (with some exceptions in Scotland). Owing to this, we have a spring, summer, autumn, and winter fishery, and it is also between the winter and spring seasons that a close time for herring should exist.

Yarmouth is the central fishing station for this great industry on the east coast of England. Wick, Peterhead, and Fraserburgh, are the great fishing stations for the east coast of Scotland, but the best fishing grounds are found on the west coast.

Immature herring, which is really summer fry seeking the ocean waters, are found in the Atlantic in vast shoals, and many fishermen traffic with these comparatively worthless fish as early as the month of April. In the interests of the Lewis fishermen alone a close time is needed, and this is asked to be from the 15th of March to the 15th of May.

From Lewis in the Hebrides, Skye, Fort William, and other adjacent districts, the boats put out for the herring fishery. Sometimes after toiling all night the boats will come home clean, but more generally the season is favourable and propitious; for instance, the records for last year (1882) "Stornoway Herring Fishing" show great success attending the fishermen's efforts. In the beginning of May for that year "shots" of from thirty to forty "crans" were very common, while several were as high as fifty and sixty-three crans. Whereas at Barra, in the Hebrides, very poor "catches" were got, at least for the opening season of that year. Again, as we shall have occasion to notice, a bad opening may end in the same place with a perfect harvest of fish, and *vice versâ*, or the season may prove a very fluctuating one at almost any station or district. Sometimes a "total failure," and often a "good season," all through the different months.

The Orkney and Shetland Isles districts follow suit, passing round the north-east coast until it (the season) reaches the central and main fishing stations for Scotland, which is early in July.

"The Herring Fishery" now takes the precedence over the "White Fish Fishery," although both are well represented from the east coast fishing stations, and it ought to be noticed that the best bait for catching our white fish is the herring itself.

Many stations on the east coast are now actively engaged from July to September, and in the latter month the northern districts are practically closed for the season, and the engagements for the east coast fishermen also end in September. For all that, the fishery is still pursued from the various stations south-east of the Firth of Forth, known as the Berwickshire Coast Fishing Stations, and large additions of mixed quality are added to the season's catch.

About this time the herrings come inshore to spawn along the coasts of Northumberland, and of course the fishermen of this part have their rightful share in the fishery, and inaugurate the autumn and winter east coast of England herring fishery.

The Tyne trawlers of Newcastle and Hull boats follow out the fishery; and with reference to the last-named town or fishing district, it may be suitable to mention at this stage a novel invention of "curing herrings by machinery," introduced by Mr. George Leach of Hull, by which he estimates a barrel of herrings can be bloated at a cost of 6*d*., as against 1*s*. 9*d*. the present cost. The plan may be described as a successive process of drying, smoking, and cooling, by carriage from the cleaning room to the grills or wire-work trays. By passing up through a series of chambers, and down again in a zig-zag direction, they are operated upon by the agency of heat, smoke, and cold, and on their coming down to the reception table at the end of the first journey, they are ready for packing.

The "Newcastle kipper" also deserves notice, as it is competing favourably against the celebrated "Yarmouth bloater" in the Metropolis, and was introduced at first by the late Mr. John Woodger, of Newcastle and Great Yarmouth.

Filey, off Flamborough Head, is the next and most important station, and exclusive of Great Yarmouth there are very large captures taken by the fishermen of Lowestoft, Folkestone, and Hastings, and boats come from the north of Scotland to share in the English fishery, although there is a winter fishery pursued in Scotland besides that of Yarmouth.

While in this vicinity we may notice the abundance of "whitebait" found during summer in the Thames, Humber, and other brackish waters near the sea coast, and that it really is the young of the herring or herring fry.

It ought also to be noticed that the smallest herrings are caught off this coast, known as "longshorers," and are really the finest caught on the east coast of England. The takes of herring by the Tyne and North Shields fishing boats for August, 1882, were so large that the "railway company had to put on extra special trains" for their transit to the Metropolis.

Coming round to the west coast, *viâ* Solway Firth and Ayrshire districts, we enter a "New Year," and they are still fishing for the best herrings that are found on any part of the British coasts. Loch Broom, Loch Horn, Loch Fyne, and many other places, have only to be mentioned, as the celebrated resorts for the best quality of herring. Indeed, during the month of October for last year (1882), extraordinary takes of herring, and such as have not been for many years, were found at Astle Bay, near the head of Ardlamont, Rothsay; from six hundred to seven hundred crans landed, and for the most part sent to England.

At Girvan, during January and February, the fishery is still pursued, and from many parts of the opposite coast, including Newhaven, fishermen come and share in the closing hauls for the season, and neither for quality or quantity can any fishing grounds equal those in the west of Scotland; but practically there is no close of the British herring fishery, although the great season is from July to September.

Yarmouth, the headquarters for the English fishery, usually commences operations at the close of the east coast fishery for Scotland. In the beginning of October, a fleet of, or more than, five hundred vessels set out to the fishing grounds. A Yarmouth lugger is better adapted for the business, and less dangerous, than the open boats of Scotland, except where the "hauling in" of the nets are concerned. This is obviated in the case of Yarmouth boats by using smaller nets, as when searching for fish the men may shoot and re-shoot them quite easily. Nets range from one hundred to one hundred and forty for each boat, and the nets are forty-eight feet long, and thirty feet deep. A Yarmouth lugger may cost from £700 to £1000, and is equipped for cargo and partial curage, carrying barrels, salt, and other essentials. The boats average fifty feet long, and the crew about fifteen men. Both the fishery and the curing processes connected with it are very carefully conducted. Buoys, in the shape of small barrels, show the position of the nets, and these buoys are painted according to the ship's name and port to which they belong, and at night lights are used to prevent collisions with the boats.

Although there is a great and increasing demand for fresh herring, especially in the earlier part of the season, the greater portion of the season's catches is cured. The broken fish is sold in hundreds of tons for manure, and sometimes at as low a figure as 20s. a ton. The curing-houses usually consist of two interior divisions, one for receiving and cleaning the fish, and the other to smoke them. The smoke-house, from bottom to top, has a series of woodwork called "tiers," on which the loaded spits hang, and the women are very dexterous in their manipulation, spitting a last in one day's time, or something like thirteen thousand herrings. Different effects follow both as to colour and curing, according to the length of time the fish are exposed to the action of heat. The names themselves indicate this, as they are called "Bloaters," "Straitsmen," "Reds," and "Blacks."

At Yarmouth, billets of oak wood are used for smoking the fish, but in the west of Scotland brushwood and furze is made use of, but in all cases of smoked fish oak wood is best for practical purposes, though pine wood is said to give the best flavour; and a great deal depends on the fish itself, and dispatch in curing them, hence the reason why the boats carry salt and other necessaries with them. The Yarmouth "bloater" is a familiar speciality, only hanging till it swells or "bloats." It is often packed and ready for transmission the night following its capture.

The Yarmouth fishermen count their herrings by "swill-baskets;" thus twenty swills make one last, supposed to contain six hundred and sixty herrings in each swill. Again, four herrings make a "warp," thirty-three warps go to a "hundred;" in other words, one hundred and thirty-two fish.

Great Yarmouth, if not itself the earliest station of which we have any record, at least occupies the sand-bank which appeared about the same time as the Roman legions. This sand-bank, "Cerdick shore," derives its name from Cerdick the Saxon, who landed here in the year 495.

Not only were the Romans great lovers of fish, but especially so to a dish of herrings, and their encampment at the mouth of the Yare still remains in proximity to

Great Yarmouth. It is said that our ancient fishermen supplied this "garianonum" or encampment with herring.

In 670 a tax upon the herring fishery is mentioned, and this tax was commonly known as "herring silver." Another reference in details is dated also with the history of Evesham Monastery, founded in 709. We also find that an annual tribute of herrings, varying from thirty thousand to sixty thousand fish, was paid as rent to one Hugh de Montford, of Suffolk Manors. The "free fair" of Yarmouth, or herring market, was attended by many foreign fishermen, and this "free fair" lasted for forty days, ending November 11th.

We have already noticed the tax paid to King Henry I., and in 1209 we find King John granting a charter to Yarmouth, on condition that the burgesses provide his Majesty with fifty-seven ships for forty days at their own charge, as often as he should need them, for hostile occasions, and also that they pay an annual fee of £55 to farm rent for ever.

The Abbot of St. Albans was a large patroniser at the herring market, and some idea may be gathered from the fact that his agents employed "seven stout and handsome horses" in carting his herrings for storage. These latter he sold over again at a profit, after the free fair was over.

Passing by many interesting records, we find that the prefix "Great" was added to Yarmouth in the reign of Henry III.; and a noble provision in Magna Charta enacted that "all merchants may with security and safety go out of England, and come into England, and stay and pass through England, by land and water, to buy and to sell, without any evil tolls, paying the ancient and rightful dues, except in time of war."

The Statute of Herrings passed in 1357 enacted, "That all herrings should be bought and sold in the haven of Great Yarmouth during the fair, not at sea, or within a radius of seven miles from the port of Great Yarmouth, and that the last of fresh herring should not be more than 40*s.*, and that two lasts of fresh shotten herring should only be equal to the last of fresh full herring.

"That all sales should be contracted between sunrise and sunset, that six score should be the hundred of herrings, and the last to be ten thousand.

"Further, that the merchants of Yarmouth and Metropolis or elsewhere sell the thousand of herring to the public after the price rate of the last, and that the Yarmouth dealers should sell the last of red herring within forty days, at and not exceeding half a mark of gain above 40*s.* paid for fresh," &c.

These provisions show how important was the acknowledged position of Yarmouth in its relations to the herring fishery.

The herrings appear on the Irish coast in June, and just at the close of the mackerel fishery, and they are captured both by the Irish and Manx fishermen. Immense shoals now commence their journey down the west coast of England, literally darkening the sea with their numbers and density. They have been known to extend a distance of six miles off the Isle of Man. Great quantities are caught in Cardigan Bay, Swansea Bay, and St. Ives Bay. It may be noticed that the west coast of England fishery commences about the same time as the east coast of Scotland, and also that the Irish herring fisheries are almost a name; for instead of working a coast that may be said to superabound with this fish, they are content to derive supplies from the north of Scotland.

Sprats (*Clupea sprattus*) are caught in abundance off the Cornwall coast, and also in the south of England; and the pilchard fishery of St. Ives is still one of the most important of any connected with the *Clupeidæ* family. The season is between August and September, and upwards of sixty years ago large quantities were caught in the Firth of Forth and other estuaries of Scotland. At present this fishery is confined to the coast of Cornwall. The mode of capture is to encircle the fish with a net called the "seine-net," requiring twenty men to each net. Including boats, netting, and gearage, the cost is nearly £1500. When cured for exportation they are carried and laid in "bulk," that is, laid in layers of salt and fish alternately, until the pile is finished. In about a month sufficient oil is extracted to allow of their being packed; and this, the last process, requires a good deal of pressing before "heading" up the casks. On this account a pressing-machine is used for three times to each barrel or cask before heading it up. The Irish coast and west of England herring fishery can show records of national importance, and charters relative to it, as far back as the year 1202.

The French herring fishery has a history of its own, and is carried out not only on its own shores, but to a large extent in English waters. Prior to the Anglo-Franco war, more than three hundred French vessels pursued the fishery at Yarmouth Sands, and at this time they were considered the best fishers in the world.

Open ruptures were common among different nationalities through fishermen trespassing in each other's waters, and in 1468 a mutual treaty was made between European powers that fishermen should be allowed to fish without hindrance in any water.

The free fair of Yarmouth drew many French fishermen,

and others likewise, to vend their produce in England. Many of the traditions connected with Great Yarmouth are strangely linked with names that bespeak French or Norman extraction.

Peter Chivalier, a Yarmouth merchant, is credited with discovering how to cure herrings in salt, and his method was followed up by one Peter de Ferars. Louis VII. of France passed an edict that only mackerel and salted herrings might be purchased at Estampes; this was in the year 1155.

It was at Kiel Bay that the food of the herring was popularly demonstrated to be of a certain kind. Although M. Mobins is not the only naturalist who has asserted this, still we are indebted to the French coast fishery for those facts which relate to herring food. In the year 1383 immense shoals were caught off the French coasts, and sometimes the schools of herring are so large that the boats are unable to take all the herring which "strike."

During the season of 1880, which was a remarkable one in all quarters, one French fisherman drew thirty-five lasts, and it is asserted that another on one occasion caught more than fifty lasts, or 700,000 herrings.

And the takes of herring by French fishermen for 1880-81 are recorded to be above the usual average.

The sprat or sardine fishery of France is the most extensive of any that seek that species of the herring; and young herring-fry and pilchards form a large percentage of the true sardine; and it may be admitted that, in other points connected with fish culture and fish acclimatization, we should do well to follow up the footsteps of France.

The herrings appear on the north-western shores of Iceland from May to September; sometimes later, never sooner, or very rarely so, and always found in September in the eastern fjords; they are never found on the south and south-west coasts.

The shoals, in their migration to the north and north-east coasts of Iceland, sweep into those fjords possessing deep water and feeding properties, and so we find them abundantly in such fjords as Eskjfjord or Seydisfjord.

The fishery is carried on in these fjords, and principally by Norwegian fishermen, who stay for the season, curing the fish at the various stations or wooden sheds erected for the purpose.

The Norwegian boats are larger than the Icelandic boats, but yet smaller than those of the east coast of Scotland.

The fishing is by means of the seine-net, and in large takes the ends of the net are anchored ashore, when the operations may now be compared to the pilchard fishery of Cornwall, the fish being taken out as they can cure them. The nets vary in size to suit the varying depths, with a mesh of half an inch.

The best kinds of white fish are found here in conjunction with the herring, besides many of the numerous enemies that pursue the shoals, such as sharks, "herring whalers," catfish, wolf-fish, sea-gulls, &c., &c., and by the end of the season, or at least in September, herring nearly one pound in weight are taken, and such usually measure fourteen inches in length. It ought to be noticed that medium herring, or even the small ones, are preferable in quality.

As stated, the Icelanders do not follow out the herring fishery, and although Norway takes a leading share in this fishery, the east coast is represented in these waters through the firm of Messrs. Slimon, Leith.

Shetland is realising the growing importance of the herring fishery, for although they pursued the cod fishery with skiffs in comparison to the open boats, or even the double-decked mainland Scotch boats, they have not only increased the number and size of the latter, but solely with the view to prosecute the herring fishery; as an instance, the following statistics will show this. In 1880, the number of boats was increased to 217. The success attending the fishermen for that year led to an increase of boats, which rose to 276 as against 217 for the year 1881; also 125 large decked boats as against 72; and in the year 1879 Shetland only possessed six large herring boats: this favourable account for this district is still on the increase. The terrible north-west gale which broke over the Shetland district on July 20, 1881, cost them the loss of ten boats and fifty-eight lives; but as many will remember, the season was a bad one all through; many valuable lives were lost, for on the east coast alone not less than one hundred and thirty-four fishermen perished within sight of home and friends. A fisherman's wife, writing about Shetland, says, " Instead of a fund for widows and orphans, could something not be done to save us being made such?"

The "haafs," or deep-sea boats of Shetland, are really what we termed them, "skiffs," barely able to carry 60 cwt. of fish; they resemble the Norwegian yawl, but having a greater spring from stem to stern.

Round the many points and promontories, and between the islands, numerous and dangerous tideways run at a fearful velocity. "Cutting the string" means crossing these tideways, and this is only attempted at slack tides; when it has to be performed at full tides, the danger will to some extent be understood; the livers of the fish are crushed to prevent the waves breaking called "lioom;" when this so-called "cutting the string" is not attempted, then they scud before the wind under bare poles.

It would prove an advantage to all connected were the

jacket-net more universally adopted at the herring fishing, as it saves time by telling whether herring are about, and at what depth, and a thermometer is also attached to show the temperature of the water.

Fishermen would be better prepared for any emergency if they would only provide themselves with a portable life-jacket, which could be inflated before taking the harbour in a storm.

Although the Norwegian schooners run to Iceland for herrings, their own fisheries, exclusive of Sweden and Denmark, are of considerable importance and value. The jagts or yawls fish in the numerous fjords, which in some cases extend inland for a hundred miles, with frowning mountains overhanging their sides, or sweeping cataracts disgorging themselves into the basin below, and sea-gulls helping themselves to the finny wealth from these waters. The depth close inshore of some fjords is one hundred fathoms, and even deeper in some cases.

The creeks of the west coast are subject to sudden squalls, which, through the intervening mountainous background, sweep down unperceived. The herring shoals sweep into and from these fjords proceeding towards Stavangar and the Naze. From Bodo and along the chain of islands known as Loffoden Islands the fishery is prosecuted, and as a feeding ground these fjords resemble our own west coast of Scotland.

Along the Swedish coast there are also rocky islands of varying length and breadth, with a fisherman's house upon one or other of them, and a creek or fissure serving the purpose of a harbour. The fishery is pursued at various seasons of the year from the Cattegat grounds into the northern Atlantic; but there are very important stations and fishing districts along the south coast, and the sprat and anchovy fisheries form an independent nucleus of wealth.

Their mode of curing is peculiar and unique. Besides curing sprats (*à la* sardine), we may get herrings skinned and boned, or skinned, boned, and marinated, that is, cooked and potted either in vinegar or glacialine, or we can get the "brack-water herring" done up in the same manner.

Perhaps we should state here that these coasts exemplify a curious feature in marine life, viz. herrings living in fresh water, being unable, through physical features of the coast, to reach the Arctic Ocean.

There are also large companies in Norway and Sweden which cure and export herrings on a very large scale, such as the Stavanger Preserving Company, Nordlands Preserving Company, Bodo, Norway, &c.

Before the eighteenth century Swedish records show that their home and foreign trade surpassed the Scottish fishery. Vast quantities were boiled down for oil, and this over and above an immense quantity consumed at home besides exportation. The same is truer still in regard to Holland, for even before the sixteenth century their herring fishery was the best developed and most extensive one known, until it was prohibited in 1625 from fishing off our coasts unless provided with a royal licence. About this time a British Fishing Association was suggested by Coke as a mutual aid in withstanding the encroachments from Dutch and French fishermen. Notwithstanding both the Dutch and French fleets continued prosecuting the fishery in sight of Yarmouth, and the Dutch fleet were guarded by war-ships. The war between France and Holland was the first perceptible step that led to a decrease in her fisheries; this was in 1702, and through which she lost four hundred of large sized Dutch busses.

The invention of curing herrings is attributed to one Beukelsz, who died in 1397, and it is recorded that the Emperor Charles V. paid a royal compliment by visiting his tomb.

It seems as if the *Clupeidæ* family had found out the truth, for some time back, in that term which is so well known, viz. "Amsterdam is built on herring bones." At least the herring fishery of Holland is not what it used to be, principally owing to the scarcity of fish, yet it was Holland who inaugurated and developed this fishery into a system of commerce, though there is good reason for giving equal or even pre-historic precedence to Scotland, who allowed it to decline.

The Dutch are famed for the scrupulous care in every incident connected with the fishery and curing operations. They have two kinds of fish and two kinds of salt; this latter commodity is brought from Spain, the barrels must be of a certain kind, the mode of eviscerating must be up to the standard, and from beginning to end every detail must be complied with ere one officer would dare to stamp them as Dutch cured herrings.

We might notice here that the word "herring" was derived from the German "Heer," an army, in relation to the moving shoals in their progress or migration.

At Nova Scotia, Newfoundland, Carolina and Virginia, and other parts of the coast of America, an extensive herring fishery is followed out, and the same physical aspects and feeding properties through the rivers and other agencies mark out these grounds as a resort for all kinds of fish.

The season for herring begins in April, when the first "run" arrives, named "Granville fish," from the course they take past that township. The May herring are spent fish, and, of course, inferior in quality. The season lasts to October, when, between the early takes of large herring, the celebrated Nova Scotia sprats form the closing hauls. Herrings of superior quality are found in the numerous bays of Nova Scotia and Newfoundland during summer and autumn, but, as we find on our own coasts, and, indeed, more or less everywhere, the herring shoals will disappear for a season, or seasons, invariably returning again to their old haunts. The sprats or herrings are cured by smoking, and one speciality in this class of cured fish is to remove the bones before drying them.

The herring species are extremely large in the North Atlantic waters. The *Clupea elongata* measures 15 inches in length and over 5 inches at its broadest part, and these, perhaps, are the extreme limits. They are very abundant during the season, and the smelts (*Osmerus viridescens*) are so abundant during the winter that they are invariably used for manuring purposes, notwithstanding their delicious flavour and edible qualities. Splendid specimens of the genus *Alosa tyrannus* are found here, and, if possible, they are even more extensively used to enrich the earth. The best specimens of our white fish are found here, and, considering the quality of their food so largely represented by the herring species, we need not search further for reasons. It is recorded that in the year 1796 a vast quantity of herring was frozen into a solid mass in one of the weirs of Nova Scotia.

As we have stated, the smallest herrings are those caught off the Norfolk coast, known as "long-shorers," and the largest specimens are found along and off the coasts of Nova Scotia, Newfoundland, Labrador, and vicinity of North America. The herring is widely distributed, abounding in the White Sea, Baltic, Zuider Zee, and in the Black and Caspian Seas. The Persians call their herring royal fish. It is a familiar favourite on all parts of the British coast, through Europe, and all parts of the northern hemisphere.

Large quantities of special cured herring are exported direct to our Australian colonies, and it is an expressed wish from the Antipodes that some effort for introducing the *Clupea harengus* be made.

Abundant as the herring is, there is good reason to believe that it may be made a common commodity wherever the conditions necessary to its habits exist; these conditions do exist particularly around the British coast, and very specially in the western islands of Scotland.

The herring is most abundant on the British coasts, in comparison to any other coast throughout the world, and perhaps this is the cause above all others why Great Britain possesses the best herring fisheries in the world.

PART II.

IN the district of Girvan there is a small village named Ballantrae, and the fishing-bed is on the "Ballantrae banks." Upon these banks the herring come regularly, and have done so for centuries, during the month of February, as a rule. This year (1883) has been the culminating point in the records of that district. Clouds of gannets darkened the immediate vicinity, or forced attention as they swooped to the surface of the water, and, rising with their captured fish, made way for others to repeat the process, in their journeys to and from "Ailsa Craig."

For the week commencing February 28th and beginning

of March, or, at least, not more than five days altogether, the total catch was "32,000 baskets," and to despatch the fresh herring, 500 railway trucks were linked on to a series of special trains. This is only for one week, and brings us already into the spring fishery, although we have yet to refer to the winter fishery. More than fifty carts were employed in taking the fish to the railway stations.

Some idea of the inconveniences resulting to our fishermen through a felt want of proper harbour accommodation may be gathered from this district.

Owing to the unsuitability for fishermen landing in this harbour they land on the beach, and when a heavy surf is rolling, this is, of course, impossible. To the credit of a few gentlemen interested in the fishermen's welfare, a machine or engine was constructed by which the boats are now drawn on to the landing-stage in safety. Notwithstanding these humane agencies, loss of life and property is frequent, and at the close of this week which we have just recorded, two Ardrishaig boats, while deeply loaded and returning from the Ballantrae banks to Girvan, ran on to the "Whelk rocks," a very dangerous reef that ought to be marked by a cage-beacon; we are sorry to add that three of the crews lost their lives, and only at some risk the rest were saved.

A cruising steamer with an officer from the Fishery Board does good service here by keeping a free course on the grounds where smacks anchor and cause obstruction.

The west coast herring make splendid kippers, and the produce of this class of cured fish comes from the Stornoway district; their fishery ends in November.

Messrs. James Methven and Company, Leith, used to take the responsibility of forwarding the kippers and cured fish to foreign ports, but, finding this too heavy for them, these gentlemen were forced to charter powerful steamers for this purpose, besides an arrangement that the Baltic line of steamers shall call at Stornoway and other fishing ports on the west coast during the season, and convey the fish to Stettin, Dantzig, Konigsberg, Riga, and St. Petersburg. Besides these large steamers, smaller craft convey shipments to Glasgow, *viâ* Hamburg, and other places, and Norwegian schooners even come for this purpose. In June for the year 1882 one steamer alone shipped upwards of 21,000 barrels of cured herring for Stettin. The smaller steamers referred to bring a large percentage of the herring to Stornoway in "bulk," to be gutted and otherwise prepared for the continental markets. The last shipment, in November, from Stornoway for Baltic ports was upwards of 1500 barrels of cured herring.

As a proof how fluctuating and uncertain the fishery may be at almost any station, we may select the present district.

At Stornoway, in May (1882), we stated that some boats realized from fifty to sixty-three "crans." In the beginning of June very poor catches were recorded, though some boats were more fortunate. Again, herrings were reported to have left the Ayrshire coast for a time, as they were met in with at the sound of Killbrannan; but one month later (September) a Troon boat came into Ayr Harbour loaded to the gunwale with a take of herring. It was estimated that she had forty maise (or 20,000 herring) of medium size and quality.

Wick, once the celebrated centre for Scotland, is a peculiar example on this point. In 1794, and even within the memory of some still alive, herrings were so plentiful that the land had to be manured with them. The selling price at Bo'ness, Firth of Forth, was 6*d.* per barrel.

Even a strong wind was sufficient to strew the beach with fish.

Some authorities assert that the diminution of the herring fishery is caused by the winter fishery for sprats and young herring, and that the same reason may be applied to our white fish; and the splendid fishery in the Firth of Forth, extending at one time to Kincardineshire, is cited as an instance how we can disperse the white fish by exhausting the herring shoals.

As good authorities assert that it is impossible to affect the herring, or cause any apparent diminution in the average takes for the season, as any differences may readily be accounted for by the season itself, such as stormy weather, not to mention the casualties that too frequently happen through loss of nets, boat, and even life itself. But since we have to close this order with the winter fishery, it may serve some purpose to examine the facts, and leave opinions alone in the meanwhile. The principal centres for the winter fishery on the east coast are Wick, Anstruther, and Firth of Forth. The Firth of Forth closes in January, and the other districts named begin the winter fishery in this month.

The statistical tables are the main guides in determining our question, and as these are appended in full for some years past, we may state as a broad conclusion that where a decrease is shown at one district, an increase is shown at another. For this year (1883) about eight yawls, which represented the winter fishery in Firth of Forth, reported very poor fishing indeed; but then the bulk of the Newhaven fleet were at Girvan on the west coast, or Anstruther on the east coast, and for both stations large takes and good prices are recorded. At Wick (1883) the catch was very small, and for the whole season up to March it records 1990 crans against 4693 crans of corresponding date of last year (1882). Now, although the comparison is very disparaging between this and last year, yet, since the inauguration of the winter fishery, the number for this year is, almost to a cran, "the number for any previous year."

This is very important in proving no diminution in the fishery itself, but, if possible, an increase, or the numbers of last year mean nothing, and, as we have tried to show, a decrease at one station may mean an increase at another.

We will now subjoin the tables for the district of Anstruther up to the year 1882. For this year (1883) a very promising commencement was made, and English buyers were early on the ground, and these were even more numerous than any previous year, representing London, Filey, Wolverhampton, Birmingham, Lowestoft, North Shields, Scarborough, Bridlington Quay, &c., and three of the principal English railway companies had representatives at Anstruther.

For the week ending January 27th the returns read

Monday	40 crans,	price 52s. to 80s. per cran.
Tuesday	200 ,,	,, 50s. ,, 53s. ,,
Wednesday	150 ,,	,, 56s. ,,
Thursday (Stormy).		
Friday	102 ,,	,, 57s. ,, 60s. ,,
Saturday (Stormy)	2½ ,,	,, 60s.

A mixed fleet of 185 boats was by the 17th of February reduced to 130, and these landed 1050 crans, realizing a sum of £3000. One boat had nearly fifty crans, and received for its cargo £130.

The 24th of February was the practical close of this fishery, owing to general stormy weather, but the details were very satisfactory for that week, and may be stated in sequence.

Monday	. . .	81 boats	400 crans,	highest price	52s.
Tuesday	. . .	194 ,,	1,288 ,,	,,	37s. 6d.
Wednesday	. .	100 ,,	400 ,,	,,	38s.
Thursday	. . .	160 ,,	500 ,,	,,	33s.
Friday	. . .	91 ,,	120 ,,	,,	45s.
Saturday	. . .	24 ,,	6 ,,	,,	92s.

Total catch for the week . 2,714

Total catch for the season, 8866 crans, or about 1650 crans above the quantity landed at the corresponding date of last year.

Now this is very satisfactory, and reads all the more favourably when stormy weather is taken into account.

CLOSE of the HERRING FISHING at ANSTRUTHER, May 1882, and COMPARATIVE TABLES for the SAME DISTRICT.

	Crans.		Crans.
1873	9,800	1878	10,500
1874	20,000	1879	2,160
1875	8,700	1880	8,630
1876	5,640	1881	16,950
1877	2,500	1882	13,380

There were nearly 1500 boats at this district in 1882, and, in consequence of competition among English buyers, the prices averaged 41s. per cran. The inshore grounds are proving more remunerative than on former occasions, and the quality superior.

Taking the winter fishery as a whole, in the upper parts of the Firth of Forth and northern districts they are very good, except for this year (1883) at Wick, which is the worst season they have yet dealt with.

The take of sprats from Firth of Forth in 1881 amounted to 13,110 crans, valued at £2786; in 1880 the take was 14,500 crans, and only realised £2175.

The chief centre for the sprat or Garvie fishery is in the Beauly Firth, and extremely heavy catches were taken in

November, 1882, as some boats had 25 crans, averaging £80 to each boat, and, as near as possible, for the whole season, £4500.

Such figures may prove very tantalising to those persons who hold that the sprat is really a herring, and, either way granted, it forms a very important item in our winter herring fishery.

TOTAL CATCH of HERRING OVER the ENTIRE EAST COAST of SCOTLAND for TWENTY-SIX YEARS; LEWIS and BARRA EARLY FISHING INCLUDED.

Year	Crans.	Year	Crans.
1857	329,251	1870	596,421
1858	393,035	1871	552,865
1859	302,943	1872	552,737
1860	463,100	1873	714,717*
1861	485,645	1874	720,964*
1862	520,280	1875	655,606
1863	439,210	1876	406,440
1864	432,064	1877	551,439
1865	395,157	1878	618,597
1866	413,065	1879	516,406
1867	474,098	1880	930,307*
1868	366,068	1881	675,107
1869	403,633	1882	730,723*

TABLE SHOWING QUANTITES BRANDED in WICK DURING the LAST TWENTY-SIX YEARS up to 30th September in each year.

Years.	Quantity Branded.	Years.	Quantity Branded.
1857	48,612	1870	38,700
1858	54,348	1871	45,700
1859	50,256	1872	42,000
1860	60,559	1873	55,000
1861	67,949	1874	51,500
1862	77,564	1875	54,000
1863	60,000	1876	36,500
1864	67,000	1877	31,600
1865	57,000	1878	60,000
1866	56,700	1879	53,450
1867	56,450	1880	77,108
1868	21,200	1881	43,046
1869	63,000	1882	48,280

WICK CUSTOM HOUSE EXPORTS FOR PAST TEN YEARS.

Quantity of Herring entered at Wick Custom House for Exportation for the past Five Years, from 1st August to 21st October in 1878, to 7th November in 1879, to 14th October in 1880, to 15th October in 1881, and to 31st October in 1882.

Continental Ports.	This series dates from 1st August to 1st October in each Year.					From 1st August to 21st October in 1878, &c., ending 1882.				
	1873.	1874.	1875.	1876.	1877.	1878.	1879.	1880.	1881.	1882.
	Barrels.	Barrels.	Barrels.	Barrels.	Barrels.	Barrels.	Barrels.	Barrels.	Barrels.	Barrels.
Konigsberg	9,508	4,277	2,883	882	3,223	2,315	1,950	8,450	3,144	4,667
Danzic	19,318	22,160	12,907	7,656	6,910	20,024	12,822	40,134	23,545	22,923
Stettin	20,492	26,130	28,630	27,466	24,063	34,122	42,427	26,666	19,232	27,854
Elsinore	3,384	1,125	..	..	..	..	..	..	..	..
Harburg	9,597	2,561	1,096	8,720	3,480	1,091	3,059	2,857	1,991	..
Rotterdam	5,493	..	..	..	..	..	..	..	..	..
Memel	900	..	..	..	347	600	954	331	..	..
Hamburg	2,915	3,997	11,314	13,898	11,230	12,229	18,982	13,425	22,704	9,606
Copenhagen	..	..	..	692	..	..	..	..	..	..
Altona	..	1,240	..	1,542	..	..	1,754	..	941	1,503
St. Petersburg	1,380	..	..	..	..	2,039	..	..	..	..
Bremen	..	..	..	..	..	410	..	..	..	..
Bremerhaven	1,150	808	..	818	600	..	..	..	..	..
Geestemunde	714	802	..	..	..	..	..	..	..	..
Libau	..	..	1,000	..	..	..	..	1,316	..	..
Emden	..	..	..	..	..	..	..	..	..	..
Odessa	..	..	..	..	..	..	..	..	..	..
Ghent	..	..	498	..	..	..	..	638	..	..
Pernaw	..	..	..	..	..	..	..	..	..	..

The above dates also apply to Irish Ports, English and Scotch Ports, for which see tables annexed.

N.B.—The above tables include the exports from Lybster and Helmsdale.

English, Scotch, and Irish Ports entered at Wick Custom House.

	1873. Barrels.	1874. Barrels.	1875. Barrels.	1876. Barrels.	1877. Barrels.	1878. Barrels.	1879. Barrels.	1880. Barrels.	1881. Barrels.	1882. Barrels.
Irish Ports.										
Limerick	..	1,430	500	850	600	1,132	..	3,085	100	..
Cork	162	2,176	2,325	3,140	1,520	1,590	1,425	..	2,110	5,870
Waterford	..	..	..	..	..	..	..	..	..	..
Dublin	..	80	1,390	2,009	..	..	240	400	850	326
Larne	..	..	..	..	..	..	..	400	..	..
Drogheda	..	..	..	..	..	..	..	450	..	..
Dundalk	450	761	1,619	..	..	..	..	..	..	..
Belfast	630	1,650	2,809	2,500	950	1,380	600	1,150	1,510	1,124
Londonderry	844	650	840	1,950	580	740	100	..	..	..
Sligo	..	880	1,210	267	..	550	..	390	552	350
Galway	..	200	439	..	..	..	..	700	450	1,378
Newry	..	340	863	..	..	..	..	650	..	..
English and Scotch Ports.										
Annan	..	..	..	..	..	..	..	..	..	..
Inverness	..	..	..	..	..	180	..	..	..	70
Stornoway	..	..	..	..	..	..	..	..	..	60
Leith	208	224	83	260	..	296	360	..	..	..
Lossiemouth	..	..	..	..	..	..	..	..	..	..
Orkney	..	..	..	..	..	..	90	..	..	..
Stromness	..	..	..	..	..	..	..	..	..	60
Kirkwell	..	..	..	..	..	..	..	315	..	..
Burntisland	..	..	..	..	..	..	..	..	..	..
Perth	50	570	355	290	..	..	..	..	..	..
Portmahomack	..	90	..	..	75	..	..	..	..	..
Tain	..	..	..	..	..	180	..	..	..	..

TOTAL CATCH at EACH STATION from NORTHUMBERLAND to SHETLAND DURING the PAST TEN YEARS.

Stations.	1873.	1874.	1875.	1876.	1877.	1878.	1879.	1880.	1881.	1882.
	Barrels.	Barrels.	Barrels.	Barrels.	Barrels.	Barrels.	Barrels.	Barrels.	Barrels.	Barrels.
Wick to Keiss	76,601	67,450	73,186	66,030	48,243	84,248	63,094	113,186	55,542	69,926
Lybster and Clyth	18,400	12,749	11,079	11,624	7,778	6,910	9,240	12,371	15,231	1,626
Forse and Forse Station	2,250	1,673	1,574	1,820	769	282	620	592	219	28
Lathernonwheel	1,965	1,045	1,468	1,785	894	512	790	637	1,237	78
Dunbeath	4,462	2,346	2,100	3,720	1,980	1,502	2,800	1,056	1,802	504
Helmsdale	5,400	5,943	3,380	8,450	13,875	7,600	10,855	10,285	13,783	3,920
Cromarty	2,754	2,400	1,551	1,166	680					
Portmahomack						858	1,391	1,790	1,515	1,376
Burghead and Hopeman	2,170	2,288	2,740	3,292	2,656	1,122	3,009	5,200	3,090	2,328
Lossiemouth	3,060	1,900	2,880	1,456	2,277	819	4,896	7,600	3,800	2,544
Buckie District	3,179	6,370	8,140	2,775	1,760	2,864	3,832	12,413	7,173	7,030
Portsoy Station	4,032	5,240	5,832	1,550	3,767	4,935	4,670	6,950	5,600	4,650
Whitehills	2,484	2,860	1,824	900	550	1,102	1,610	1,667	840	1,174
Macduff	11,360	15,860	11,360	2,208	3,840	4,756	7,384	8,530	5,538	9,762
Banff		1,520	3,026	1,014	810	250	1,360	1,913	1,606	3,030
Gardenstown	12,200	8,850	3,400	2,680	5,874	4,058	7,007	6,915	7,685	4,387
Fraserburgh and District	157,415	181,060	196,838	87,776	150,280	175,820	105,037	218,504	132,613	139,500
Peterhead District	168,000	164,294	128,556	72,045	85,440	122,456	83,200	177,300	124,800	124,185
Aberdeen	60,690	64,900	61,104	57,149	77,000	69,231	36,400	78,810	78,657	80,253
Montrose District	37,945	38,135	39,017	25,327	38,925	26,758	30,048	54,091	45,352	28,820
Anstruther and District	4,305	1,930	300	110	3,005	3,975	6,490	7,840	3,660	3,145
Eyemouth " "	31,228	24,900	29,200	15,600	11,250	25,407	52,149	48,715	59,486	59,825
Dunbar*	1,170	4,968	1,155	620	800	1,500	5,460	4,600	4,110	2,722
North Sunderland	12,250	23,904	15,000	15,000	10,850					
Orkney	19,950	20,389	12,196	4,843	9,776	14,722	8,364	16,142	14,418	16,160
Shetland						6,240	6,700	38,700	46,250	102,000
Lewis and Barra	73,450	57,100	39,900	12,700	74,240	50,670	60,000	94,500	41,100	45,240

N.B.—Stonehaven has been disjoined from the Montrose district and become a separate station. The results for the year 1882 are therefore given separately.

* Leith added to Dunbar in 1878.

The herring is a very voracious feeder, and, according to M. Mobins, the principal food of those found in the Baltic and German Ocean consists of some kinds of minute crustaceans of the order of *Copepoda*.

In February, 1872, a number of herrings were caught in Kiel Bay at about 240,000 herrings daily for three weeks, and in almost every one that M. Mobins opened, the stomach was found loaded with *Copepoda* belonging almost entirely to one species (*Temora longicornis*). By careful counting the number present in one case was found to be 60,895, and another herring contained 19,170. The upper surface of the water swarmed with these animalculæ, and could easily have been taken with fine nets in literal thousands. A very low estimate was assumed from these facts, namely, that allowing each of the 240,000 herrings to have devoured daily 10,000 *Copepoda*, this would give for one day a consumption of 2400 millions, and in three weeks 43,000 millions.

The roe of an ordinary sized herring is allowed to contain about 33,000 eggs, and the time taken for hatching the eggs depends both upon the season and the temperature of the water. Hatching operations seldom take longer than one month, and the young fry are invariably produced from the eggs in three weeks' time.

As with all our marine fish, temperature has a very important function in the growth and development of each species, and observation is showing a close relation between large or small catches and varying temperatures. Thus a low temperature is conducive to large catches, and a high temperature to small ones, and if the thermometer registers the sea temperature to be at or about $55 \cdot 5°$, average catches may be expected, other things being equal.

One of the most serious allegations against trawlers is,

that they both disturb and destroy immense quantities of herring spawn, and a very recent instance was cited by the Cockenzie fishermen and laid for redress before the Lord Advocate at Edinburgh, urging him to draw attention to this and other grievances they have to suffer. This is a public question, and may be dealt with at some length. The allegation was that a trawler brought up an immense quantity of herring spawn, and that it was sold for "manure." This is an old story, for the same complaints were made against the English trawlers, and at a commission of inquiry appointed by Government, it was alleged by a South Shields fisherman that he had drawn up himself three and a half tons of fish-spawn, and further, that he has seen a ton and a half of herring spawn offered for manuring purposes.

It is important to remember that up to the present date there is no diminution, but, as we think, rather an increase in the herring fishery; for all that it behoves us, for the future interest of our sea wealth, to make the strictest inquiries from competent sources and legislate accordingly. More than fifty tons of herring have been taken at one haul, and, considering the constant drain at all times of the year by the varied enemies of the herring, there is reason enough to feel anxious about the future welfare of our herring fishery.

The report of the Fishery Commissioners issued in 1879, estimates that 120,000,000,000 of herrings are annually destroyed by men, birds and fishes around the British coast, but that 1,200,000,000,000 eggs are deposited in the sea as a balance against this draught.

It is a fact that fifty years ago large quantities of fine herring could be found as far up the Firth of Forth as Alloa, and the curing troughs still remain along the coast as a sad evidence; but it could not have been the trawlers who prevented herring ascending the Forth, seeing that they are a recent innovation on the east coast fishery for Scotland, and it is interesting to find that the Newhaven fishermen have launched a trawler for themselves, as of all, perhaps, they had most reason to complain. That the trawl will bring up herring spawn there can be no doubt, but, as a rule, it cannot do so, for herring prefer spawning among rocks or upon coarse ground, where the trawl cannot go without injuring itself.

Again, trawlers assert that our flat fishes are the most voracious feeders upon herring spawn, and that, as they capture a large proportion of these fish, they are really conferring a benefit upon our fishermen by its use.

A counter allegation was, that the use of circle trawls instead of ordinary beam-trawls in the sprat fishery enabled the fishers to capture young herring, and that the destruction of these young fry was fatal to the white fish fisheries and conducive to a diminution of the herring themselves.

A very important point comes out in connection with the Firth of Forth, and one which we have already alluded to, namely, that herring became scarce in this district before the introduction of trawlers. If it can be shown that there is no decrease on other parts of our coast where trawling operations are carried out, then the question is so far satisfactorily settled, and we think the statistics are on this side. But there are some very important reasons why specified limits as to the kind of trawl to be used, and the place or grounds to be fished over should be rigidly maintained. The law at present seems to be a dead letter in many points, and this is chiefly owing to a felt want for marine police. It is a frequent occurrence for trawlers to run right through the nets, and it is at any time dangerous for them to be in the vicinity of open boats using either nets or lines.

Trawling cannot be abolished without an international convention, nor is it generally desired that it should be even without this; but that some effective measures which will meet all cases is requisite, and urgently demanded, the baneful system of coopering alone will show. A cooper is a floating public-house, under the colour of a fishing smack. The worst is that these bumboats sell or barter poisoned drink in return for fish; and cruel evidence has been proved against this villainous traffic, where in many cases not only do they take all the money first, but have as often succeeded in securing fish, nets, gearage, and even the boats too, in return for a maddening drink that has made some victims leap overboard through its effects. Evidence of a worse nature than this was brought against foreign fishermen, chiefly Belgian and Dutch trawlers, to the effect that not only were the nets purposely run through, but the warp was cut in a deliberate manner by an instrument called the "devil." This instrument resembles the end of a huge scythe, and when fixed at the stern of the ship it can be used with terrible effects to the helpless fishermen.

International protection is both needed and asked for as a guarantee against these nefarious proceedings, for the regulations at present existing only apply to territorial waters, and the application of the law is the fault at issue. Even where ordinary grievances prevail fishermen can raise an action for damages, but as a rule they have neither opportunity nor means to do so. Some useful remedies have been often suggested, such as empowering our coast-guardsmen at their respective stations to act on the complaint of a fishing crew, or to have at least four swift cruisers in the German Ocean, representing England, France,

Belgium, and Holland. Also, with a proposal to adopt fish culture in some of our favourite estuaries and firths, that trawling be entirely abolished from such districts, &c.

It is now five hundred years since a petition was presented to the English Parliament against the use of a machine which not only retained all kinds of fish, both small and great, in the meshes of its net, but also by its iron supports destroyed fish, spawn, &c., "to the great damage of the whole commons of the kingdom." Trawling, then, has not yet reduced the fish supply, and it only now remains to guard against this.

Much of the so-called herring spawn has been proved to be gelatinous bodies of marine zoophytes and ascidians, or the spawn of cuttle-fishes, but, as we stated, herring eggs have been brought up by the trawl.

The old legal mesh for the herring net was 1 inch square from knot to knot, but since 1868 fishermen have been allowed to use any size of mesh they please. It is desirable that the old law of 1809 be re-enacted, because a small mesh will catch small, and therefore young, herrings; at the same time it can only choke large herrings without catching them. There are very many points which require overhauling in the interests of the fishermen alone. And there are some which require redress in the interests of the public. For instance, boat owners and others "sailing by the share" must proceed in the first instance to a custom-house, and sign their respective contracts before the officials. The charges for taking depositions as to damage or loss at sea should be from some other source than the sufferers themselves.

Great damage is done to nettage by lost anchors ripping them open, and these hidden snares are unintentionally encouraged by the Board of Trade, for heavy penalties bind the salvors to deliver "swiped anchors" to the Receiver of Wreck. Now, as very few owners return to look for lost anchors, and the amount given by the Board of Trade for salvage is extremely small, it follows that very few take the trouble to clear the grounds, notwithstanding the general loss continually accruing.

Again, if statistics are to be taken at all, they should be dealt with generally all round the coast, either in the order of the fisheries themselves, or commencing in the north and ending in the south, or where practicable. Statistics for the east coast of England are always awanting, and when given very unreliable as a total estimate to the growing importance of the English coast fishery.

The spring herring fishery at Lowestoft is a recent addition to this industry, but usually the largest deliveries of the season are landed at Yarmouth. It is asserted that in 1853 upwards of 10,000 lasts of herrings were cured at Great Yarmouth. And it is within the estimate to allow the yearly average to be 15,000 lasts delivered at Great Yarmouth alone for the past thirty years. One authority assumes the grand total for the past thirteen years to be at least not less than 2,772,000,000 herrings, or 210,000 lasts.

Before noticing the leading fishery and particular features connected with it, a novel and very pleasant pastime is offered to anglers through the open facilities in catching herrings. A few enterprising individuals have even supplied the markets by angling operations over the side of a boat, and others have taken them from the shore itself. The reason why this mode of fishing is not more general than it deserves to be, is the erroneous ideas existing about the fishing apparatus and habits of the herring. Herrings are a surface-swimming fish, and the great point to successful angling is the smallness and brightness of the hooks used, as the herring possesses a very small mouth. In the north of Scotland some anglers fix the hooks from the end of ordinary stocking wires, and these wires are about twelve inches distant from each other on the line. No bait is required, but the hook must be small and bright.

PART III.

The Leading Herring Fishery of the World.

As the herring fisheries of Scotland are the leading fisheries in the world, we may infer from this fact alone that there must be gigantic modes of carrying on the business in the mighty waters.

The curers are the real promoters of this industry; in some cases they even provide the boats and gearage; but arrangements are made long before the season begins, notwithstanding the fact that the fishery is to a large extent uncontrollable by regulations. Thus, though boat-owners may bind themselves to deliver a certain number of crans at a given time in the season, it is after all a probability that these very men may have the "cleanest" boats for that season.

The "bounty system" is a mode of advancing money, and as often a question of retaining it, and cannot be compared to the "share" principle, where the fishermen have a better compensation for their arduous work. Boat-owners try to strike as good terms as possible, and by stating an agreement entered into last January (1883) for the ensuing season, we may illustrate this.

Herring Fishing Engagements at Broughty Ferry, January, 1883.

Twenty-one boats, with the crews already made up, are arranged to fish as follows:—Montrose district, ten boats; Aberdeen district, nine boats: the other two to fish between or on the coast bounded by the Tay and Montrose. Terms, £45 of bounty, £1 per cran of fresh fish for a complement of 200 crans, and 15s. per cran for salted herrings. Arles, money or perquisites in addition to each boat's crew, £2. In the case of the Montrose boats the herrings will only be considered fresh when landed at 1 A.M. In the case of the Aberdeen boats the herring will only be considered fresh when landed at "midnight." After these hours the prices allowed will be the same as is allowed for salted fish, &c.*

The highest prices are paid for the early takes in every district; and as it would be noticed, the men are bound down to a given time, even should their boats be so loaded that they cannot get in.

Enormous quantities of early fresh fish are trucked immediately to English markets, or partially cured and shipped to German ports, till at length the curing yards become a scene of life and activity that can only be compared to the herrings themselves in their onward progress beneath the waves.

The largest quantity exported from any Scotch port as a cargo was that of last season (1882) by the ss. *Silesia*, from Peterhead, with 3075 barrels of cured herrings, and at present Peterhead and Fraserburgh are the leading centres of the east coast for Scotland, just as Great Yarmouth and Lowestoft are in England.

For Fraserburgh the season's cure of 1882 is very close

* It may be stated that the bounty is better this year by about £10 than on any previous occasion.

on the numbers of 1881, but both the vessels employed and the exportations show an increase, thus—1881, vessels employed, 158; 1882, vessels employed, 173. Or to tabulate it in fuller form, thus :—

Fraserburgh.		Fraserburgh.	
Season 1882.		Season 1881.	
Vessels employed for conveying cured herring to continental ports—		Vessels employed in 1881—	
Total number	173	Total number	158
Barrels exported . . .	160,678	Barrels exported . . .	145,494
	Barrels.		Barrels.
July	28,914½	July	29,845½
August	63,574½	August	39,297
September	47,321	September	40,053
October	20,131	October	22,800
November	..	November	12,496
December	..	December	620¼
January	736½	January	...
February	..	February	382
Totals . .	160,677½	Totals . .	145,494

· The second section of tables gives a comparative view of the Monthly Shipments under their respective dates to various continental ports.

The curing process begins at once, and for this purpose all hands are ready to begin work. The herrings are counted out by the cran to the curer; the cran is a measure holding forty-five gallons. The "gutters" or eviscerators immediately commence to open and clear away the intestines. These persons are usually women, who work in gangs of five or eight at a time. The fish are carried to the "rousing troughs," where, as the name implies, they are roused in salt, and so expert are the women at cleaning, salting, and packing, that they will produce a barrel to the cooper in ten minutes with ease.

When large takes of herrings come in it is necessary to

have many hands at work, for, unless the herrings be in pickle the same day of arrival, the officer will not brand them, or at least is supposed to see that this requirement is fulfilled.

This brand question has been a bone of contention and source of controversy for many years, and it is unfortunately branded itself by many fishermen and large curing-firms as a useless and misleading system, and the question has now come to be whether it should be retained or dispensed with. The old Scotch Fishery Board was established in 1808, but it seems probable that this vexed question may be successfully handled by the re-arrangements of the Fishery Board of 1882. As the case stands, the duties of the Board are the branding of the herrings according to quality, together with a collection of statistics as to the fishery itself.

Many of the firms who stand upon the merits of their own productions have a strong case in point of various classes of cured fish, which at the same time would not be unimpaired by a British brand, and, to say the least, would look all the better.

The Stettin Herring Report for last season, dated November, states that the supplies of Scotch herring brings the import up to "85,553 barrels crownfulls, against 87,238 barrels in 1881; 48,751 barrels unbranded fulls against 32,377; 46,112 barrels crown matties against 50,902; 42,213 barrels unbranded matties against 30,829; 7802 barrels crown and unbranded mixed against 5921, and 12,482 barrels crown and unbranded spents against 13,279; 3656 turnbellies in barrels against 2,919—246,559 barrels in all, against 223,465 barrels in 1881.

"This year's import is now considerably larger than the total of last year, and will be still increased by about

10,000 barrels floating for our port; but the stocks of Scotch herrings are not all large here, in fact, considerably smaller than last season, the consumption having been very satisfactory."

The herring is known as fry or sil, matties, fulls or full-herring, and spents or shotten herring.

The matties are the finest condition of the fish, when all the food goes to form the fattening properties of the fish. A full herring is a later stage with the milt or roe fully developed, which is not the case with matties; and, as the name implies, a spent or shotten herring is one that has spawned.

The herring is a very symmetrical fish, and its distinguishing features are the head and the belly. Although there are no eyelids, yet the eyes are large and extremely beautiful. It possesses all the characteristics applying to such fish as were enjoined as edible food in the Scriptures. It has seven fins, and the number seven is the perfect number in Scripture, and these fins are respectively—dorsal, 1; pectoral, 2; ventral, 2; anal, 1; and caudal, 1.

Strange markings may be seen beneath the delicate scales, which are compared by fishermen to a herring-net; indeed, some assert that the idea was conceived from this as to how a net should be constructed; fancy might rather attribute this to the first herrings which escaped from the nets, and the impressions they received would be indented in their whole being, and handed down to future generations. And when the mouth closes, so as to allow the cheeks to overlap the lower jaw, certain well-defined outlines are seen on each side, which fishermen say resemble a fishing-boat with the mast in the very position it should be when the men are engaged in fishing operations. The air-bladder is joined both to the vent and stomach. The vertebral column has fifty-six bones. The ribs consist of twenty-one to each side. The head is furnished with twenty-eight bones, eight of which form supports to the gills. From end to end the entire skeleton numbers three hundred and seventy-one bones, and in this form it presents a marvellous view of constructive skill and adaptation to its home in the great deep, and reflecting the mind at once to that supreme source from which order has sprung.

The order of the fisheries just given will indicate the habitat of the herring, and it is never found in warm latitudes, though often found both in and without the Arctic circle. Small varieties are met with on the northern shores of Greenland, and it is scarcely necessary to state that the annual migration of herring shoals to and from polar regions is now known to be a fallacy. It is found in the North Atlantic Ocean between forty and seventy degrees of latitude, and abounds in the northern seas, and found in greatest numbers on the British coasts.

The herring is not so prolific in the produce of spawn as many of the other species are, unless we take into account that it may spawn oftener than other fishes; and this is a point that many able men are still investigating. It is estimated that if the full-roed herrings recorded as taken for the year 1881 had been allowed to spawn, and if that spawn had become fry, then "there would have been produced no less than 6,946,470,000 barrels of herring," had such been caught. This assumption is very modest, and, of course, is going on the old lines that the said full-roed fish would only spawn once, though they spawn at least twice in the year; and it seems certain that they spawn much oftener, as both "spent" and full herrings are caught in nearly any season and at any place. The fact really seems to be that, once they come to maturity, it is only a question of regaining their strength after spawning as to when they shall spawn again; and it is not improbable that the fecundity of the herring is much greater than it is commonly supposed. When accurate knowledge is established on such important points as these, then our dominion over the fish of the sea will have attained its highest degree, "for knowledge is power." There is also good reason for believing that what is generally called a white sea by fishermen is really produced by the innumerable presence of herring spawn and herring fry, as such are actually found upon the surface of the waters in thousands, and many think, despite the fact that herring eggs are found at the bottom of the waters, that they are really produced and vivified at the surface. Indeed, some fishermen think that it is owing to the non-impregnation of milt and roe that eggs are found at the bottom at all, and that only those eggs float which have been so impregnated; if so, this places the herring on the same footing with our other white fish in regard to its breeding points.

The report of the Fishery Commissioners for 1878 states that 2,400,000,000 of herrings are annually caught in the North Sea by the British, French, Dutch, and Norwegian fishermen, and it is estimated that Scotland alone possesses no fewer than 14,500 herring-boats, with a total for men and boys of about, or more than 50,000, and statistics show that these numbers are increasing every year as yet.

Surface fishing is an improvement on the old method, and proves that the herring are nearer the surface of the water than was usually supposed. This method is conducted with great success, and consists in letting the back ropes be lowermost, so that the bottom of nettage may float towards the surface; but this plan is open to great risk from passing vessels.

Experienced fishermen are usually able to shoot their "nets" at the right time and place, and they can even sight and fix the spot for operations at a distance, as the schools of herring will often throw an oily phosphorescent gleam along the surface of the water. There are other indications as to the presence of herring, and often enough the nets are shot at a venture. Some Norwegian fishermen use water-glasses in their coast fisheries; this is a simple instrument that enables them to see a long way into the depths, and is probably only a practical aid at such places as the fjords or inshore fisheries. When the train of nets has been cast into the sea by being paid over the stern of the boat as "she" is rowed slowly from the starting-point, then a great perforated wall is left in an upright position on which the shoals will strike in their onward progress, and thus be taken prisoners.

The beautiful tinted silver rays produced as the herrings are emptied into the boats baffles all description, but the curing-yards are now the only thoughts for the fishermen with their silver treasures, for this may be the last haul for the season, and, as we have been there already, we may now take leave of the "Herring Fisheries," and, as we say good-bye, we wonderingly inquire, if all the herring-nets in the world were joined together, where would they reach?

"Who can tell?"

International Fisheries Exhibition,
LONDON, 1883.

THE

HERRING FISHERY.

BY

R. HOGARTH.

[*PRIZE ESSAY.*]

LONDON:
WILLIAM CLOWES AND SONS, Limited,
13 CHARING CROSS, S.W.
1884.

THE HERRING FISHERY.

IN the early history of our nation the North Britons were fonder of the chase, or an occasional raid by night on salmon with torch and spear, than looking after the treasures of the deep.

Little is known of herring except that the Dutch visited our coasts annually for the purpose of fishing them, returning often with good harvests. It is difficult to understand why Britain did not cultivate such an important industry, allowing the Dutch to have it all to themselves, unless it was the many wars she was engaged in and the continual local feuds that kept her hands full, for it would appear that this branch of fishing was very little followed after till the middle of the seventeenth century, and even then it remained for a long time unproductive, for many reasons, of which I will mention a few : first, the fishers were nearly all small crofters, who, as they derived their subsistence chiefly from their crofts, did not require to prosecute the fishing to any extent. If they earned as much as would pay their rents and get a few necessaries that their land did not supply, they were content ; and as they lived a very frugal life, their wants were but few. *Causes of the neglect of fisheries. Unproductive even in 17th century. Reasons.*

Another reason was that their materials were not good. The boats that were used for fishing did not suit the *Materials defective.*

Boats (their build, &c.). purpose well, being nearly half as broad as they were long, and open from bow to stern. There was no place of shelter in them, nor any way of cooking their food. Oars were always used, but the fishermen always carried a large blanket with them, which served both as a covering to keep them warm and a sail when the wind was fair. These boats were round-sterned—from fourteen to sixteen feet keel and about seven feet beam. It was not possible to go any distance to look for herrings in boats of this description. They were known by the name of "nabbies."

Nets and their manufacture. The nets were also very indifferent, being all home-made. The women spun the twine, and it was very coarse, twice as heavy as that used at the present time. The fishers themselves made the nets.

Crew. There were generally four men in each boat, and each boat carried a train or fleet of nets consisting of four barrels, **The term "barrel."** one for each man, the name "barrel" arising from the habit of carrying their nets in barrels when going from one fishing station to another. The barrel or net was not made in one length; it consisted of thirty "deepings," each deeping being twelve yards long and fifty meshes deep, the size of the mesh being rather more than an inch, or what we term thirty-four rows per yard. I will now proceed to make some general statements, confining myself to the west and north coasts of Scotland.

The method of fishing is nearly alike as regards herrings on all the British coasts, except "trawling," which I refer to **Opinions of writers regarding migratory habits of herrings.** afterwards. Buffon and other writers were of opinion that the herring was migratory, that our coasts were wholly supplied from the Arctic regions, and that herrings visited our coasts in spring and left in early winter. The spawning **These opinions contradicted.** banks off Ballantrae and others around our coasts have proved the fallacy of these opinions. In regard to these statements, I remember hearing an old legend told, how that herrings were only to be found on the east coast of Scotland ; so a silver herring was made and towed after a vessel or boat round Cape Wrath, and the whole shoal followed and filled all the west coast. *An old legend*

I do not doubt that we get a supply of herrings from the oceans around, but I think we depend chiefly on the herrings bred in our own waters. Men of experience seeing herrings in any of our markets can generally tell where they are caught. *Herrings from the oceans around. Distinctive marks in herrings of separate localities.*

Herrings fished at different places have their own peculiar appearance, such as Loch Nevis, large ; Loch Hourn (6 or 8 miles distant), small ; Scalpa, large ; Loch Broom, small ; Hebrides, all large ; Loch Fyne, generally large ; and Firth of Clyde, generally small. *Places quoted.*

This grouping of herrings in different classes according to size proves, I think, that each class of herring frequents its own particular locality. I may state that I noticed in a newspaper that one of our professors had examined herrings caught at the Hebrides, and found that they had one or two more joints in the backbone, and one or two more ribs in either side, than herrings caught near the mainland. This shows that there is a difference in the species. *The herring scarcely migratory.*

In the early history of the herring fishing there were sometimes great quantities caught, although the boats and nets were deficient. The fishermen waited till the herrings went to the heads of the lochs in shallow water, where their capture was easy. Sometimes their nets were so full of herrings that their boats could not take more than half of them. But that involved no loss, as they could return when empty and haul the remainder. Nothing could go wrong with their nets, as they were generally trammelled in *Great quantities caught occasionally in early times.*

Carries built. sheltered places. Carries were built in some places, that is, a round circle was built with stones to the height of about four feet. At high water the tide overflowed the wall by some feet, and the herrings went in and got ebbed.

At Loch Slaben in September 1867 one hundred crans were taken in one of these old carries that had been kept in repair.

The beginning of this century. About the beginning of this century there were large fleets of vessels, of from 30 to 150 tons burden, fitted out from our ports on the Clyde bound for the lochs in the west and north highlands to buy and cure. Others of them fished their cargoes. The herrings were all sold by the cran—a cran holding forty-five gallons.

Price and profits. The average prices at the fishing stations were from 10s. to 15s. per cran.

Great profits were realized, as they were seldom sold in the market at less than £2 per barrel, and sometimes at a much higher figure. It was one of the staple trades of *A town built on herring-bones.* Greenock, and Rothsay is said to have been built on herring-bones. Ayr and other places contributed their *Saltcoats.* fleets. Saltcoats, a small sea-port, sent out twelve to twenty vessels every season.

The varying fortunes of the trade. The vessels that bought generally made a good many runs in the season, if the fishing was good. Sometimes it proved a complete failure, and it was not an uncommon thing for a vessel to come home clean. I remember hearing of a vessel and her two fishing boats being away *Government encouragement.* four months, and all for one barrel of herrings. Seasons so poor caused heavy loss to all concerned, and the Government saw that a branch of our industries was not *Board of Fishery.* improving. So they established a Board of Fishery, with powers to give grants to fishermen and to maintain law and order among them. One of the grants allowed was for the purpose of helping to repair broken boats. They offered a bounty for herrings fished a certain distance from shore. This deep-sea fishing, however, did not succeed, as fishermen had not made any improvement on their materials. *(Government superintendence of fisheries.)*

At that time there was a heavy duty on salt, but salt used for curing herrings was relieved from taxation by Government. They also stationed fishery officers at the different fishing districts along our coasts, to look after fishermen's interests, and to settle any disputes among them, or between them and the buyers. They were there to see that no measures were used except those that bore the Crown brand. *(Fishery officers appointed. Their duties.)*

If herrings were sold by the hundred, forty-one casts and a tally were given, making in all one hundred and twenty-four herrings; this was the rule on all our coasts except at Howth, where forty-two casts were given, being three herrings more. If there was anything too difficult for these officers to settle, they referred it to headquarters. They were also experienced in curing, and had power to brand barrels, first having ascertained that they were well filled and properly cured. Curers who wanted the Crown brand had to pay a small fee for each barrel. Crown brands always drew a better price in home and foreign markets than individual or company brands. The Government also appointed a revenue cutter under the Board to attend the fishing fleet. Her duty was to see that each boat was properly lettered and numbered. These letters are the custom-house initials of the district to which the boat belongs. *(Higher price drawn by Crown brand. Revenue cutter and her duties. Lettering and numbering of boats, and the advantages of the same.)*

The letters and numbers have proved very useful if any damage is done, such as fouling of boats or destruction of nets; the guilty parties can at once be found, if their official number is known, by applying to the cutter. At the outside fishing stations she goes to sea every night along with the fishing fleet, not returning till the fleet is in harbour, and if any boat gets disabled she takes her in tow.

Cutter goes to sea with the fleet.

The fishing gradually improved under the Fishery Board, but it was not until about 1840 that a new epoch in the history of the herring fishing came about, when a Mr. Paterson patented a machine for making nets. He opened business at Musselburgh, and it was not long before he had a great many machines at work. The demand for these nets was very great, and has gone on steadily increasing. There are now a great number of these net factories over our land and our colonies, and other parts of the world are supplied with these far-famed nets. The machine nets are much fairer than those made by the hand, and consequently fished better. Instead of two hundred meshes, as before, they were increased to three hundred meshes deep, and in two or three years the trains increased in some cases to twenty pieces, each piece a hundred yards long and three hundred meshes deep. By this time there had been a great improvement on the boats. There was the "wherry," a good large-sized boat with a place for the crew to sleep in, but rather clumsy on the whole. The fishermen began to see that these boats were, although better than their predecessors, still unsuitable, and that they required something faster and abler. So they applied to Mr. Fife, boat-builder, Fairlie, father of the present Mr. Fife, yacht-builder there, who built a number of beautifully modelled fishing boats, some of them being 39 feet keel, 12 feet beam, and from 6 to 7 feet depth of hold. A plan was also invented for lowering the mast when the nets were shot, allowing them to be hauled much more easily. These boats sailed very fast, and suited our waters well;

Improvement under Fishery Board.

Improved nets.

Difference between hand and machine-made nets.

Nets enlarged.

Better boats, but not quite adequate.

Superior boat from Fairlie.

Plan for lowering sail.

THE HERRING FISHERY.

but for the outside fishing nothing has yet been found to equal the Penzance and St. Ives luggers. I consider them far superior to the east of Scotland luggers; the fineness of their lines and the symmetry of their hulls make them more to resemble pleasure yachts than fishing boats. Some of our west of Scotland fishermen went to England and got boats of this class built to order, and their models were copied here for the mackerel and outside herring fishing. When fitted up with every appliance they cost nearly a thousand pounds. Our fishermen say they are really good boats, being so buoyant that they can weather almost any storm. The Isle of Man fishers seem to have a like good opinion of them, as all the old crafts have given way to them. The nets in these large boats are nearly all hauled by spring-backs, which are hove in by capstans or winches. Some of the largest boats indeed employ steam winches for this purpose. There is an improved winch, or, as fishermen call it, "iron man," which can be used without a spring-back, thus saving both labour and expense. The east coast fishermen regard it as a great improvement. The boats used at both the out and inside fishing are in the best of order, and whatever may be said to the contrary, the gear, sails, sleeping berths, cabins, &c., are all good. Speaking of boats and their furniture, I may state that it has often occurred to me that a part of the ballast carried on the outside of the boat would prove a protection against capsizing, and give more stowage for nets. That this would give extra speed is shown by the example of the yachts. Some people might object to this proposal on the ground that it would be unsuitable for dry harbours, but I cannot think that a few tons of iron bolted through the keel and through a good keelson would do any harm; and where the boats were always kept afloat, more could be added. I mention iron as

[margin notes: Penzance and St. Ives boat. Adopted in Scotland. Cost of these boats. Nets in boats mentioned. "Spring-backs." "Iron man." Boats and furniture in good order. A suggestion.]

being much less expensive than lead, and a casting of iron of the required mould could be made at any foundry.

Steamboats for fishing herring. Steamboats for fishing herrings have been tried, but on account of the expense involved have hitherto been little better than failures. However, I think I am safe in saying that steam will yet become general in our herring fishery. When such improvements are being made in the departments of steam and steam engines, it is difficult to say what may not be in the future.

Steam fishing boats of great service at outside fishing. Steam fishing boats would be of great service at our outside fishing grounds, which are sometimes far from harbours. The fleet sometimes goes as far as thirty or forty miles to sea, and then calm weather or headwinds are great drawbacks, especially with heavy hauls on board, as if they are not in time for that day's market the whole cargo is generally lost, and likewise the following night's fishing. I have seen, both at Stornoway and at Howth, as many as two nights' fishing lost in one week with calm weather.

Towing at Shields. At Shields towing is becoming very common among the fishing fleet; a tug will engage to attend six fishing boats for a week for £30—£5 for each boat—thus showing that steam for herring fishing is much required; and it is to be hoped that, seeing steam trawlers have been so successful in other fishings, it will not be long before steam will be employed in this fishing also.

The year 1848 nets. Cutch. Tanning of nets. Returning, in the matter of nets, to the year 1848, I may first mention that cutch was for some previous years used by fishermen in tanning nets, sails, &c. It is a great improvement on the old system of boiling oak or larch bark to draw the tanning qualities from them. I have seen days and nights occupied under the old system in doing an *Advantages of "cutch."* amount of work that with cutch can now be done in as many hours. The cutch has only to be melted in water and poured on the nets in a large tub till they are well saturated. This process is repeated once a month while the nets are new, afterwards the periods can be lengthened; but if nets have not been properly cured they will rot in a very short time. *Method of tanning by cutch.*

Different substances, such as alum, oils, dyes, tar, have been tried for curing purposes, but nothing has yet been found to equal cutch.

Small trawl-nets were in use before the year I have mentioned, chiefly for fishing saithe. When these fish came close to the shore a few herrings were sometimes caught in this kind of trawl, but they were not looked after. About this time a fisherman belonging to Tarbet on Loch Fyne lost part of his drift-nets, so he made a large trawl of what remained. *Trawl-nets for "saithe."*

The first night he went out he secured a large haul of herrings with this net, about four hundred maise (five hundred herrings being a maise). This was a turning point on the road to improvement in our herring fishing, proving in this case the truth of the old adage, "Necessity is the mother of invention." *Trawling for herrings commenced.*

About this time a number of fishermen, the writer being one, began to make trawl-nets. In the beginning of 1849 I had in one haul upwards of three hundred crans of very large herrings (about five hundred to the cran). We drew, however, only a very small price for them, about 5s. a cran, as we did not know of any fresh market for them, and curers were afraid to buy, as they thought that trawled herrings would not cure. One buyer sent a few of them to England, and next year the result was that we had buyers from different parts of England, including London; prices rose to 7s. and 8s. per hundred, or from 35s. to 40s. per cran, showing that there must have been a great demand for large herrings in England. *The writer's experience in 1849. English market opened. Its beneficial results.*

Before this the buying was mostly in the hands of the curers. The greater part of the herrings fished on the coasts of Scotland were cured and sent to the market and sold as new salt herrings. Grocery shops and other places of retail sold them by the pound, like any other commodity. The opening up of the English market to us, and the prices realized there, alarmed the curers, who thought this new method of fishing would hurt their trade, and they raised the hue and cry which several interested parties were not slow to take up. They said that trawling would soon rob our waters of all the mother herrings, and that herring fishing would soon become a thing of the past. Among the malcontents were fishermen, if we can call them fishermen—men who earned their livelihood as such in the summer months and returned to their trades or farms in the winter. In the newspapers articles appeared against trawling, and monster petitions, very largely signed by consumers, were presented to Parliament against the practice. The consequence was that in 1860 an Act was passed making trawling illegal on the west coast of Scotland, also closing the time for fishing herrings from the 1st of February to the 1st of June.

Many fishermen and their families were brought to poverty through this Act. The law was so strictly enforced that the fishermen were not allowed even to fish herrings for bait, and a substitute for this purpose could not be found. Her Majesty's Government at last became aware that some error had been committed and appointed a Commission to investigate. The Commission found that neither the quantity nor the quality had been produced since the passing of the Act already referred to; it was repealed as soon as possible and all restrictions removed. After this herring fishing began to flourish. Cotton twine was also introduced for making nets, giving us a finer, cheaper, and more durable article than the hemp or flax nets that were formerly used.

Trawling has now become a recognised method, and the nets are enlarged to such an extent that, instead of being fifteen or eighteen score meshes deep, they are now from forty to fifty score meshes deep, and three hundred yards in length. *Trawling now a recognised method. Trawl-nets.*

Some of our fish merchants tried a small screw-steamer to attend trawlers and run with their herrings to the market, as heavy hauls were sometimes got early in the morning. This plan succeeded so well that we have now about a dozen screw-steamers in attendance. Tugs are sometimes chartered for the same purpose. These steamers are all capable of maintaining a high rate of speed, some of them reaching eleven or twelve knots an hour, so that when they get their cargo of herrings on board they very soon reach Glasgow, often before the market is open. If the herrings will suit the English market they are sent off per rail as soon as possible, and will arrive in England in good condition. When the steamers are on the fishing ground they follow the fleet, and the fisherman who gets a good haul shows a signal with a light which the buyer understands. A steamer is soon on the spot, and when the price is agreed on, the work of transferring the herrings from the boats to the steamer is soon accomplished. The herrings are sold by the basket to further their dispatch. *Small screw-steamers employed by merchants. The herrings transferred from boat to steamer.*

It requires two boats for trawling, and each boat has a crew of four men. They generally put to sea in the afternoon to look for appearances. One man is always stationed at the bow to keep a look out, and the practised eye will at once detect the slightest appearance of herrings. *Two boats for trawling. The "look-out."*

There are different ways of discovering their whereabouts, sometimes by the presence of gulls, "gannets," porpoises, or the whale. But what is most depended on is what fishermen term "putting up." Bubbles are seen rising to the surface caused by the water passing through the gills of the herrings. The other appearances mentioned are often on small fry, but this of "putting up" seldom fails. When seen the net is run out in the form of a half circle and hauled near the shore, if possible. The two ends of the net are hauled into the boat, forcing the herring into the centre or bag, where they can be taken out with baskets. Heavy fishings are also got in the middle of our channels by making a circle with this net. I think that steam launches would be a benefit for trawling purposes, as the boats are too large to be easily managed with oars, and they could go a greater distance in calm weather to look for herrings. The take with drift-nets on the west of Scotland has been greatly on the increase for the last two or three seasons, while in Loch Hourn it has been unprecedented.

Our east coasts both in England and Scotland have also done well, and good "takes" have been fished at the Orkneys. Some of the boats fished there two hundred crans in a few weeks. At Howth and Ardglass it has fallen off greatly, and no reason can be given for it. It cannot, however, I think, be attributed to over-fishing. In my own experience I have observed that herrings will frequent certain grounds for a number of years, then suddenly leave, to return again when not expected.

An improvement has of recent years been made on the drift-net which I cannot explain better than by saying that the net is turned upside down. The strong rope is underneath, and a small cord or rope is run along the upper edge well corked, so that the net can be kept on or near the surface. This plan will do well where herrings are fished in the tracks of steamers. Some of these, as well as sailing vessels, draw twenty-four feet water, so fishermen must have their nets fully that distance below the surface to allow them to pass; so if the herrings are near the surface the greater part of the nets will be beneath them. When the small rope is uppermost, steamers or sailing vessels passing over the nets will only break the small rope, doing very little damage, as the strong rope will keep the whole fleet of nets together. By this means the herrings can be fished near the surface. This inverted net was first used on the east coast of Scotland, where it has now become general. A few of the west coast fishermen have adopted the plan with success. *Inverted net first used on east coast of Scotland.*

At Ballantrae a different kind of net is used when the herrings are on the banks spawning. These nets are called 'bottom nets," and are about eighty meshes deep. A rope is put on both edges; the upper one is well corked, while on the one underneath stones are tied to keep the nets at the bottom, the stones being some distance apart. A large stone is attached to either end for moorings. I have seen these narrow strips of nets completely filled with herrings, and when this is the case it is with the greatest difficulty that the crew can get them hauled. *Nets at Ballantrae. "Bottom" nets.*

It is to these banks that the greater part of the herrings on the west coast of Scotland resort to spawn, and I may add from the English Channel also, as great shoals are seen coming from the south. The herrings begin to gather there about the 1st of January, and by the middle of February the greater part of the body has arrived. They begin to spawn about the end of February, and are generally spawned and away by the middle of March. *Banks at Ballantrae. Spawning.*

Herrings do not go in a body after spawning, but scatter, keeping near the surface to get food, and if it is mild weather they are in good condition by the middle of June.

Ancient origin of Ballantrae fishing.
Its importance.

The Ballantrae fishing is of long standing—some old papers turned up not long ago showing that herrings were fished there as far back as the 15th century. But it is only of recent years that it has become of such importance. As many as five hundred boats from different parts are fishing there every season; the majority are trawling, and the greater part doing well, as the prices are generally good—much better than in the summer season. The most of these herrings are sent per rail to England.

Fishing at spawning time.

Some think that herrings should not be fished when near spawning, as it will affect our future fishing, and that they are not in a good condition for food. Regarding the last statement I would say that the prices realized for them show that they cannot be in a bad condition, and the idea that man may reduce the quantity of herrings in the sea is simply absurd. As many as 68,608 eggs have been counted in a single female, and if only a tithe of them would come to maturity our waters would get completely filled.

Herrings the food of other fish.

All sorts or kinds of fish in our waters will eat herrings, and they constitute the chief food of the most of them. It is enormous the amount of herrings destroyed by other fish for food. I saw a fish caught about twenty lbs. weight, and in its stomach were one hundred small herrings about two inches in length. Now if a single fish will consume that quantity at one meal what must the total consumption

Sea-fowl also live on herrings.

be? It is well known that sea-fowl also live almost entirely on herring, so that the herrings fished by man must be only a small fraction compared with what is destroyed otherwise.

Abundance of herrings at Ayr, 1796.

I remember seeing in an old Edinburgh publication that on the 20th of August, 1796, the herrings were so plentiful along the shores at Ayr that the people got a good supply by means of baskets. This is not at all wonderful, as three years ago we lifted a good many on board with baskets in deep water off Ballantrae. *Abundance in recent years.*

Writers differ widely in their opinions regarding the time required to bring a herring to maturity—most of them thinking that it takes years. Fishermen, too, I observe, are undecided on the point, but recent experiments in Rothesay Aquarium will throw some light on the subject. Herrings put in there a few inches long became full grown in less than eighteen months, though they did not fill properly. It may be supposed that if in confinement herrings grow so quickly, maturity must be reached much earlier in the open sea, where proper food can be got. At Ballantrae, in 1879, I assisted Mr. Melville, who was fishery officer there at that time, in procuring some herring spawn for the late Mr. Frank Buckland, Her Majesty's Inspector of Salmon Fisheries. He wished to ascertain the time taken by the herring to arrive at maturity. Most likely the spawn died before reaching Mr. Buckland, as his investigation was unsuccessful. The bottles employed were small, holding only two pints or little more. These were filled three parts with water, and pieces of seaweed to which the spawn had adhered, were also put into the bottles, which were closed by covering their mouths with thick paper secured with gum, no air being admitted. The spawn would be at least two hours out of water before being placed in bottles. Had larger bottles been used, the spawn placed immediately in them and the cover perforated, the result might perhaps have been more satisfactory. It is very beautiful to see the spawn on a broad leaf of seaweed. There is no crowding, each egg or particle is placed in the nicest precision, and there is ample space to allow the egg to expand as the young herring is *Maturity of the herring. Rothesay Aquarium. Growth of the herring. Mr. Buckland's investigation. A failure. Probable causes of the failure. Beauty of spawn on seaweed.*

Early development. forming. I have seen head and eyes distinctly developed five or six days after being spawned.

Growth of herrings. If their growth could be ascertained as easily as that of the salmon, it would most likely be found that the herring, to arrive at maturity, takes months instead of years, as is generally supposed at present.

Two classes of herrings. It is universally thought that there are two classes of herrings, the "Gutpock," or herring that feeds, and the herring that derives its nourishment from water only. All herrings, however, must eat till they are full grown, and after spawning they eat till they become "prime," that is, when *Stomach.* they become well filled with fat. If this fat was examined the stomach would be found in the centre of it, completely closed up.

Weather—its effects. I believe that warm weather is beneficial for fishing, especially in summer, as heat is requisite for bringing to *The food of herrings.* life that small fry on which herrings feed. This fry is scarcely discernible, but when sailing over a quantity of it the water has a reddish appearance. It is generally near the surface, and if drift-nets are run out through this, good fishings are generally got if herrings are there in search of their food.

Personal experience. In my own experience at different fishing grounds I have always found that the stomachs of prime herrings when *Food of herrings.* examined were empty, and that their general food was that small animalculæ which I have just referred to, and which, depending on the warmth of the season, is to be found in the end of April or the beginning of May. This animal- *Summer life.* culæ or crustacea comes into life with the increasing heat of the water, and dies when the cold comes, the quantity always being in proportion to the degree of heat. Another *Jelly-fish.* instance of this short summer life is to be found in the jelly-fish, which appears in the beginning of summer affords food and shelter to the young whiting, and dies on the approach of winter. A warm summer must therefore, as I said before, have a beneficial influence on the fishing, as it is generally the end of summer when herrings become "prime." *A warm summer beneficial.*

If, however, the herrings cannot get this food, which appears to be specially prepared for them, they will take shrimps or other small fish. It is in August that our lochs teem with herrings, especially our deep-water lochs, and it is there that herrings get that fine flavour for which Loch Fyne herrings are so much famed. When fishing in Loch Fyne I have seen the nets lowered twenty, forty, and even fifty fathoms below the surface to get these fine herrings. In Loch Hourn and all other deep-water lochs along our coasts the herrings improve in quality very rapidly. About August herrings gather into large bodies, and if broken up they immediately close again so as to protect themselves against their enemies. These shoals can only be attacked on the flanks, as when alarmed the body becomes so dense that the assailant is in danger of being choked by the multitudes. It is for such shoals that trawlers naturally watch. If they are not seen in the daytime by the appearances I have already described there are other ways of finding them at night. If it is a moonlight night fishermen watch eagerly for them rushing or "putting up" on the surface of the water. *Other food. Deep-water lochs. Density of shoals. The shoals and the trawlers. "Putting up."*

But when the night is dark, a man is stationed on the look-out, and by striking on the gunwale of the boat, the herrings can easily be seen moving by means of the phosphorus that is in the water. If herrings are plentiful they will make such a flame that it will light up all around the boat when a heavy stroke is given on the gunwale. I saw a statement by one of our professors, to the effect that he had examined the head of a herring and that it con- *A dark night. Phosphorus.*

tained no organ of hearing. If this be the case the other senses must be very acute, as at the slightest noise they will swim away, though it be a gun fired at a considerable distance. The same appearances are, of course, looked for by drift-net fishermen.

Herring having no organ of hearing.

It is in the evening that herrings generally "mesh," before the "fire," as the fishermen term it, comes into the water. The reason of this is that herrings notice the nets by the phosphorescent light and avoid them. If the fishing is light and the night long the fishers generally haul in their nets and look somewhere else for herrings, so that they may have another chance before the break of day. It is different altogether when there is moonlight, as then herrings often net all night. Hence the line in the old song, "The herring loves the merry moonlight." Drift-net fishermen have many enemies which prey on the herrings caught in their nets. During some seasons the "dog-fish" is very plentiful, and very destructive, doing great damage to the nets as well as abstracting the herrings. Porpoises too, in large numbers, frequent our waters, and, when they discover nets well-fished, the fishermen have but a poor chance, as the nets are cleaned by them faster than they can be hauled. There are many other enemies among the large fish which do a great amount of damage, but the most destructive of them all is the basking shark or sunfish. It visits our coasts in the beginning of summer and leaves at its close. Fishermen greatly dread this monster, as it often carries away their nets when it gets entangled in them, or if the nets are left they are so badly torn that they seldom can be mended.

Morning fishing.

Fishers change their positions.

Moonlight fishing.

Enemies of fishers.

Dog-fish.

Porpoise.

Nets attacked.

The basking shark.

Destruction of basking shark among nets.

Harpooning the "shark."

In the beginning of this century the harpooning of the basking shark was common on our coasts, and it is said to have been very remunerative, as an immense quantity of oil as obtained from its liver. I mention this because I think that not only would it be profitable to pursue this fishing at the present day, but it might help to rid the waters of one of the drift-net fisherman's worst enemies. It may be the scarcity of the fish was the cause of this fishing being discontinued, but its reappearance in greater numbers during the past ten or twelve years might warrant fishermen in turning their attention to the subject. It would not be difficult to harpoon these fishes, as they will remain on the surface a long time, allowing a boat to come up quite close to them before going down. *Harpooning the "shark" recommended*

Having just returned from Ballantrae (March 20, 1883), I will add my experience of the year's fishing there. It was the general opinion of all fishermen that there were more herrings on the Ballantrae Banks than had been there during any previous season in their experience. The gales, however, in January and February were very much against the fishing; it was but seldom that boats could go to sea, and when they did get out it was only with the drift-net that boats did any good. I have explained before that the trawl boats have to be pulled with oars while making a ring, and the drift-nets are run out in a straight line before the wind, consequently there were very few herrings landed, and prices ran as high as £5 per cran. The 1st of March brought a change for the better, and there were landed on one day seven thousand crans; prices ranging from 15s. to 20s. per cran, mostly trawled. Some of our trawlers are engaged by an English firm to trawl during the first two months of summer on any part of the Irish coast from Innistrahull to Ardglass. They are to be attended by steamers to take the herrings to market. The trawl has never been used before in this district for herring fishing. *Experience at Ballantrae. Year 1883. Gales in January and February. Drift-nets only of use. Price. Improvement in March. Engagement of trawlers for Ireland.*

Shetland and the trawl.

In conversation with some fishermen who had been fishing among the Shetland Islands during last summer, I heard it stated that trawling, if adopted there, would be a success, as the herrings were close inshore. The only difficulty would lie in getting the trawl boats there, on account of the great distance.

Source of wealth to England.

I need not say anything here of what a great source of wealth the herring fishery is to our country, as that is well known from the figures published regarding our exports, not to speak of the immense quantities consumed at home. It would not be possible to give a correct statement of what is used at home; there are so many bye-ports and creeks where herrings are landed.

"Catch" greater.

It is acknowledged by all, including those who would put restrictions on engines used for fishing, that the "catch" of herrings is greatly on the increase.

No danger of reduction of supply.

I have forty years' experience, and I see no danger of reducing the quantity of herrings in our waters. All the improvements on our material have been a benefit both to fisher and consumer, and, judging the future by the past, we may expect greater

Better methods in future.

improvements and better methods still in capturing the finny tribes. Restrictions on any industry are hurtful, but they are particularly so when applied to herring fishing.

Curing.

Before closing I may mention that the system of curing for the home market is now nearly supplanted by better methods of preparing herring for food. There is the

"Bloater," "kipper," &c

"bloater" and the "kipper," and many other ways of making them more palatable than having them packed in barrels and covered with pickle.

Railways.

Our railways are also a great advantage to fishers, branches being laid to all the principal parts of the coast, and steamers run in connection with them to the islands, bringing as it were the remotest stations near, so that

England can in a few hours get a fresh supply from the far North.

It is computed that in Scotland alone upwards of one hundred thousand persons depend on the fishing for their support, and if England and Ireland were added thereto, the number would be immense. It is well known that our navy derives a great many of her seamen from our fishing population, and so does our merchant service, proving that Great Britain's fisheries are most beneficial to her, both directly and indirectly. *Number of persons dependent on fishing. Benefit of fisheries for the navy.*

Our Government has always taken a deep interest in the fisheries of the country, and fishermen as a rule know this and appreciate it. They are a loyal race, and, if need be, they would, in the words of the poet:— *Government's interest in fishing. Loyalty of fishers.*

> " Stand
> A wall of fire around our much-loved isle."

www.ingramcontent.com/pod-product-compliance
Lightning Source LLC
Chambersburg PA
CBHW020900230426
43666CB00008B/1249